# That I
## May Know
# HIM

*The Never Ending
Passionate Adventure*

**Keith Pointon**

WestBow
PRESS
A DIVISION OF THOMAS NELSON

WestBow Press books may be ordered through booksellers or by contacting:

WestBow Press
A Division of Thomas Nelson
1663 Liberty Drive
Bloomington, IN 47403
www.westbowpress.com
1-(866) 928-1240

ISBN: 978-1-4497-9235-0 (sc)
ISBN: 978-1-4497-9234-3 (hc)
ISBN: 978-1-4497-9236-7 (e)

Library of Congress Control Number: 2013907533

Printed in the United States of America.

WestBow Press rev. date: 05/02/2013

# Table of Contents

# Philippians 3:10,11

That I may know him, and the power of his resurrection, and the fellowship of his sufferings, being made conformable unto his death; if by any means I might attain unto the resurrection of the dead. (KJV—King James Version)

to know him, and the power of his resurrection, and the fellowship of his sufferings, being conformed to his death, if any way I arrive at the resurrection from among the dead. (J.N. Darby)

that I may know him and the power of his resurrection, and may share his sufferings, becoming like him in his death, that if possible I may attain the resurrection from the dead. (RSV—Revised Standard Version)

That I may know him, and the power of his resurrection, and the fellowship of his sufferings, being made conformable to his death; If by any means I may attain to the resurrection of the dead. (R Webster)

I long to know Christ and the power which is in His resurrection, and to share in His sufferings and die even as He died; in the hope that I may attain to the resurrection from among the dead. (Weymouth)

to know him, and the power of his rising again, and the fellowship of his sufferings, being conformed to his death, if anyhow I may attain to the rising again of the dead. (Young's Literal Translation)

How changed are my ambitions! Now I long to know Christ and the power shown by his resurrection: now I long to share his sufferings, even to die as he died, so that I may perhaps attain as he did, the resurrection from the dead. (JBP—J.B. Phillips).

*I want to know Christ and the power of his resurrection and the fellowship of sharing in his sufferings, becoming like him in his death, and so, somehow, to attain to the resurrection from the dead. (NIV—New International Version)*

For my determined purpose is that I may know him—that I may progressively become more deeply and intimately acquainted with him, perceiving and understanding the wonders of his person more strongly & more clearly. And that I may in that same way come to know the power outflowing from his resurrection [which it exerts over believers]; and that I may so share his sufferings as to be continually transformed [in spirit into his likeness even] to his death, [in the hope] that I may attain to the [spiritual and moral] resurrection [that lifts me] out from among the dead [even while in the body]. (Amp—Amplified Bible)

*Yes, for his sake I have been caused to forfeit all things, and I count them but dung, in order that I might come to know Him in an experiential way, and to know experientially the power of His resurrection and a joint-participation in his sufferings, being brought to the place where my life will radiate a likeness to his death. If by any means I might arrive at the goal, namely the out-resurrection from among those who are dead. (KW—Kenneth Wuest)*

# Foreword

There is an adage which says, "It's not what you know but who you know." Having served the Lord for over sixty years in various leadership capacities, I can testify that I have proved the theme of this book, *That I May Know Him*, to be the heart and core of the gospel.

The old hymn puts it simply, 'Knowing Jesus is all that matters; your life will never be the same.' The big question is how well do we know Him? That's the subject this book explores.

I have known Keith Pointon for over four decades and been blessed by his ministry. I recognise him as a ministry gift of Christ to the church as a 'helper' (1 Corinthians 12:28). Many remember and still appreciate his gifting in music leadership. He has also served the Lord in multiple administration capacities such as treasurer, missionary agent, and the ability to get alongside others to encourage them. His service carries with it a quality which is often lacking.

Keith operated in the latter years of his working life in a self employed capacity and this book is a sequel to what happened in a difficult period during that time. This led to a deepening of his walk with the Lord and eventually resulted in his retiring early to prepare for his next, as yet unknown, stage of his life.

A few years after retirement, at a time when most people are considering taking things easy, Keith and his wife, Anne, found themselves obeying the call of the Lord to serve him for two years in China followed by the same period in the Philippines.

At this time Keith and Anne are back in the local church scene and are also significantly involved in ministry in two local prisons.

I am sure that, as you read this book, you will find it to be challenging, chastening and encouraging.

Thank you, Keith, for sharing your heart: help us to open ours.

Peter Cochrane
Assemblies of God in Great Britain (Scottish Area).

# Preface

It's true to say, and I'm speaking from experience here, that our greatest growth points in God are brought about during difficult times. When things are going well the natural gravity in our lives is to become somewhat complacent and self sufficient. We read how that works when we see God's dealings with Israel in the Old Testament. It's a paradox, but within God's blessings seem to live the seeds of apostasy and we need to keep watch over our lives in easier times for their germination.

At the end of 1986 I was in a bit of a crisis as far as business was concerned but it was a crisis that started me on an exciting adventure which I'm still enjoying and finding challenging twenty six years on. It started when God gave me a specific call to learn how to listen to him in greater depth, but more about that in chapter nine. This book has come out of that process.

The basis of this adventure has been simple—I sit down with my bible, God's word, and the Holy Spirit and read. I don't consult the notes in my study bible nor do I use commentaries etc. It's just a relaxed, unpressurised time spent with the Lord. It's not a time for presenting requests to him or bible study as such, just a matter of learning to recognise the voice of the Shepherd. It's the highlight of my day and I guard that time jealously; it underpins my whole life.

I've progressed over the years into greater intimacy with Father, Son and Holy Spirit and it's a process that is still going on, yet the thrill is still as real as ever and the Holy Spirit continues to draw me further in and opens my understanding.

I trust that, as you read this book, you too will experience a greater desire to deepen your walk with the Lord and that it will, perhaps, also confirm and encourage you on your existing journey.

God speaks to us in so many ways but I've found that the most powerful, real, consistent and upbuilding way is through his word. I trust that, as you read these pages, it will be the passages from Scripture that will impact you most. They're reproduced in full so that you can read them without interrupting the continuity of the narrative. Read them carefully, prayerfully and unhurriedly and experience the voice of the Shepherd. If the only benefit you receive from reading this book is a fresh impetus from the bible my writing of it will have been worthwhile.

## Event versus process

There are many events in life, most of which seem fairly mundane. There are, however, some that seem much more exciting and are looked forward to with great anticipation. Events, whether pleasant or unpleasant, can be just that, a one-off affair, or they can have a more lasting effect. Ideally each event should be built into a life process to produce personal growth in us.

What that means is that we take at least one principle from that event and use it to take us to a new level of personal development. When we do that intentionally and consistently we find that, despite life's ups and downs, our general trend is upwards, leading to increasing maturity. My hope and prayer for each reader is that you take at least one principle from this book and make it part of your life process. If that happens it will fulfil, in large part, my purpose for this book.

Unless otherwise stated scripture quotations are from the New International Version. The key to abbreviations are incorporated within the various translations of Philippians 3:10, 11 at the beginning of the book.

Keith Pointon

# CHAPTER 1

# Foundations

When constructing a building there are three very important principles which need to be followed. I'm sure there are more, but three will do here.

1. The quality and strength of the building are directly related to the quality and strength of the foundations. You cannot put more into your building than the foundations allow; the higher the superstructure, the deeper the foundations.
2. There is a correct, logical order in which the building work must proceed. In other words, you can't put on the roof before the walls, and you can't put up the walls before you've laid the foundations.
3. You can't rush certain procedures. For example, you can't move in heavy plant until the concrete floor has fully set and achieved its optimum strength. Nor can you skimp on the quality of the materials used.

If we don't lay this foundation thoroughly our building will be flimsy and very limited. It may look good initially, but is it the real thing? Is it genuine all the way through or is it more like a Hollywood film set? It looks good for the cameras, but go round the back and there's nothing there.

1

This foundation, which is the basis of everything in our Christian walk, is all about the closeness of our relationship with our heavenly Father and his Son, Jesus. It's also about our walk with the Holy Spirit. Everything we are and do as Christians flows from this source. Whatever does not flow from our intimacy with the Lord—be it worship, preaching, teaching, practical service, or anything else—has very limited spiritual, eternal value. In fact, without intimacy the Christian life is about as fulfilling and exciting as watching grass grow.

A good many years ago (almost forty at the time of writing), when I was pondering my Christian life, and how I felt that something vital was missing, the Lord highlighted Philippians 3:10 to me. In those days I used to read the King James Version, so here's the verse from the King James Version.

> *That I may know him, and the power of his resurrection,*
> *and the fellowship of his sufferings....*

It was like a light going on, and that verse set the course for my life. Having said that, I've got to admit that progress was slow and very spasmodic for many years, but in the last few years there has been a great acceleration towards this goal. J.B. Phillips, in his translation of Philippians 3:12-14 expresses it like this.

> *My brothers, I do not consider myself to have "arrived", spiritually,*
> *nor do I consider myself already perfect.*
> *But I keep going on, grasping ever more firmly that purpose for*
> *which Christ Jesus grasped me.*
> *My brothers, I do not consider myself to have fully grasped it even now.*
> *But I do concentrate on this: I leave the past behind*

*and with hands outstretched to whatever lies ahead*
*I go straight for the goal—*
*my reward the honour of my high calling by God in Christ Jesus.*

I want to share with you in this book some of the insights I've gained on this journey, this journey of passion.

# CHAPTER 2

# Intimacy—the First Priority

I think that the most important reality to grasp at the outset is that God desires intimacy much more than we do. He walked with Adam every day, just to have fellowship with him. God wasn't looking for a gardener or zoo keeper; he could easily have chosen names himself for the animals, and keeping the garden in trim wouldn't pose any problems for him.

Although God and Adam would discuss the work that Adam was carrying out, that wasn't the main purpose of these daily walks. God's purpose was for fellowship with Adam for the sheer joy of it. He had created Adam to have fellowship with him and to express himself through him.

This is what we were made for, and without close fellowship with God we've missed it. *This is the bottom line.* This is what it's all about, not doctrine or serving, not following rules and regulations (which can creep up on us unnoticed). No, God wants this fellowship to be restored. He wants to walk with us continually. He wants to become real to us—up close and personal. Salvation is all about a restored relationship.

But all that was lost through sin, and it broke God's heart. That intimate fellowship between God and his son, Adam, was severed, and I'm sure that one of the emotions that the Father God felt as he called Adam was one of great sorrow. "Adam, where are you?" was not a question because God didn't know Adam's whereabouts, but a cry of anguish at his loss. We'll look at this later on.

There were those in the Old Testament who caught something of God's heart in all this. We read in Genesis 5:24 for instance about Enoch, who "walked with God; then he was no more, because God took him away."

## Moses—A man face-to-face with God

Moses was another man who had an understanding of God's heart, and he longed to experience this intimate walk with God. He did, in fact, walk very closely with God, and Exodus 33 is a startling example of how important fellowship with God was to Moses. For me this chapter is one of the pivotal ones in Scripture.

Moses had just been up the mountain to get the Ten Commandments, and when he got back down he found an orgy in full swing. There was even idol worship, a golden calf, which had just emerged from the fire by magic when the Israelites threw in their gold, according to Aaron. Now that takes some believing.

God is understandably extremely upset at this and tells Moses in no uncertain terms what he intends to do.

> *"Go up to the land flowing with milk and honey.*
> *But I will not go with you, because you are a stiff-necked people*
> *and I might destroy you on the way …*
> *… Tell the Israelites, 'You are a stiff-necked people.*
> *If I were to go with you even for a moment, I might destroy you.'"*

So that's the end of that then, Moses; we'll get you there, but with an angel instead of me. You'll have a successful ministry, but without my presence.

What would you have done in those circumstances? Here's Moses' reply in verses twelve and thirteen:

> *Moses said to the* LORD, *"You have been telling me,*
> *'Lead these people,' but you have not let*
> *me know whom you will send with me.*
> *You have said,*
> *'I know you by name and you have found favour with me.'*
> *If you are pleased with me,*
> *teach me your ways so I may know you*
> *and continue to find favour with you.*
> *Remember that this nation is your people."*

Then in verses fifteen and sixteen he says this,

> *Then Moses said to him,*
> *"If your Presence does not go with us, do not send us up from here.*
> *How will anyone know that you are pleased with me*
> *and with your people unless you go with us?*
> *What else will distinguish me and your people from all the other people*
> *on the face of the earth?"*

Now we've got to remember that at this point Moses didn't know how this conversation was going to end. He was a prophet but not that prophetic! He hadn't yet written the end of this chapter, so, as far as he was concerned, he could be consigning himself to spending the rest of his life in this howling wasteland with a bunch of constantly complaining people. And he would never complete the job (the ministry) he'd been called to do.

For some people their work, their ministry, is their significance. Take that away and they've nothing left of value. This was some decision that Moses had to make.

But God knew what was going to happen, and he was testing Moses as to his hunger for himself. I'm sure that the Trinity was filled with joy when they heard Moses' reply. Here was one of their creation who wanted God just for who he was, not what he could give. And here's the reply Moses got (verse fourteen):

> *The LORD replied, "My Presence will go with you,*
> *and I will give you rest."*

Please notice that Moses wasn't going to be put off easily, because it was after God had said this that Moses insisted that God go with him. It's obvious from verses fifteen and sixteen that the most important thing in life to Moses was God's presence, and his tangible presence at that, as we'll see shortly. So in verse 17 the Lord gives his commitment to Moses.

> *And the LORD said to Moses,*
> *"I will do the very thing you have asked,*
> *because I am pleased with you*
> *and I know you by name."*

What an answer, and what an affirmation for Moses—"I know you by name." But Moses wasn't satisfied with even that affirmation; he goes on (verse eighteen),

> *Then Moses said, "Now show me your glory."*

You could say that Moses was hungry for God, a God Chaser, as Tommy Tenney would put it. And God answered Moses' request as far as it was possible for him to do so. What an experience for Moses to have, as described in verses nineteen to twenty three.

*And the* L<small>ORD</small> *said,*
*"I will cause all my goodness to pass in front of you,*
*and I will proclaim my name, the* L<small>ORD</small>, *in your presence.*
*I will have mercy on whom I will have mercy,*
*and I will have compassion on whom I will have compassion.*
*But, he said, "you cannot see my face, for no-one may*
*see me and live."*
*Then the* L<small>ORD</small> *said,*
*"There is a place near me where you may stand on a rock.*
*When my glory passes by, I will put you in a cleft in the rock*
*and cover you with my hand until I have passed by.*
*Then I will remove my hand and you will see my back;*
*but my face must not be seen."*

I don't know about you, but I'm never satisfied with just the facts. When I read accounts of what great men and women have done for God I'm as much interested in what God had done *in* them in secret as he has done *through* them in public. You see, what we do, if it's going to be effective, is merely a flowing out of that hidden, secret life which has taken many years of costly experience to bring to maturity. Merely saying the words or copying the actions doesn't have the same effect.

Why can two people say the same thing and with one it will be like dynamite, whereas with the other it will be more like a damp squib? That's because with one it's the distillation of the inner, hidden life, and with the other one it's merely copying someone else. I was talking to someone recently about the same principle, but in a different application, and he said, "What you have is only the karaoke version." What is vitally important is our 'secret history with God', that eight ninths of the iceberg that's never seen. It's the hidden part of us that determines what kind of people we really are.

In her book *Intimate Friendship with God,* Joy Dawson puts it like this,

> Our ministries are marked with authority only to the degree that the life of the Lord Jesus is the only explanation of what comes forth from us. This is possible as we consciously, wilfully, lean on the Person of the Lord Jesus Christ in faith to do in us and through us what we're totally convinced we cannot do ourselves. We simply say, 'I can't, but You can, and will now. Thank You," and take the next step of obedience. His supernatural life is then released according to our need.

So I'd like to know *why* Moses acted the way he did. What motivated him to take such risks? We don't have to go far to find out—only as far as verses seven to eleven in the chapter we're looking at.

> *Now Moses used to take a tent and pitch it outside*
> *the camp some distance away,*
> *calling it the 'tent of meeting'.*
> *Anyone enquiring of the LORD would go to the tent of*
> *meeting outside the camp.*
> *And whenever Moses went out to the tent,*
> *all the people rose and stood at the entrances to their tents,*
> *watching Moses until he entered the tent.*
> *As Moses went into the tent, the pillar of cloud would come down*
> *and stay at the entrance, while the LORD spoke with Moses.*
> *Whenever the people saw the pillar of cloud standing*
> *at the entrance to the tent,*
> *they all stood and worshipped, each at the entrance to his tent.*

> *The L*ORD* would speak to Moses face-to-face,*
> *as a man speaks with his friend.*
> *Then Moses would return to the camp,*
> *but his young assistant Joshua son of Nun did not leave the tent.*

I think those verses say it all. An angel was no substitute for God's presence at these regular meetings. Only meeting face-to-face with God would satisfy Moses, God himself speaking to him face-to-face like a friend. "You can keep your successful ministry and your angel, nothing can substitute for intimacy with you," is what Moses was saying. The rest of his life in the desert with intimacy with God was worth infinitely more than getting to the Promised Land.

What was it Paul said in Philippians 3:8?

> *I consider everything a loss compared to*
> *the surpassing greatness of knowing Christ Jesus my Lord,*
> *for whose sake I have lost all things. I consider them rubbish,*
> *that I may gain Christ …*

The focus of Moses' life was intimate fellowship with God, not achievement, ministry or success. That's what gave direction to everything he did, it was the colouring of his life. It was the determining factor for everything that mattered. He hadn't always been like that; there was a time when his achievements were what mattered, but forty years looking after sheep changed all that.

I like what Sammy Tippit writes in his book *No Matter What the Cost*.

> Moses' life would never be the same after His encounter with God. His heart was set apart for God's divine purpose. He became known as the friend of God. Exodus 33: 11 says, 'The L*ORD*

used to speak to Moses face-to-face, just as a man speaks to his friend.'

Too few people are known as the friends of God. Many are known as great communicators and ministers, great musicians and workers. But a great need exists for friends of God. A friend of God will have the imprint of holiness on his heart and the tool of prayer in his hand. He will live every day with a separated and seeking heart. Many claim to have a seeking heart without having a separated heart. They claim to pray and seek God but continue to live with sin tucked away. They may fool others and may even deceive themselves. but they will never fool God. Only a holy heart will be honoured in the presence of a holy God.

## David—A man after God's own heart

Let's take a look at King David for a moment. He was described as 'a man after God's own heart' (Acts 13:22), yet he was an adulterer, a liar and a murderer! So how can we describe him as this man after God's heart?

As I said earlier, what's important is to look at what's behind the external appearance, the heart of a man. How has God dealt with him, what's his secret history with God? Happily for us David has revealed much of his heart to us. All I want to do here is to quote some of the things David said which reveal his heart.

*You have made known to me the path of life;*
*you will fill me with <u>joy in your presence</u>,*
*with eternal pleasures at your right hand.*
*Psalm 16:11*

> *Seek the Lord and his strength,*
> *yearn for and <u>seek his face</u>*
> *and to be in his presence continually.*
> 1 *Chronicles 16:11*

> … <u>*know*</u> *the God of your father—have personal knowledge of him,*
> *be acquainted with him and understand him;*
> *appreciate, heed and cherish him—*
> … *if you <u>seek him</u>—inquiring for and of him*
> *as your first vital necessity—*
> *you will find him …*
> 1 *Chronicles 28:9 (Amp) (addressing Solomon)*

> <u>*One thing*</u> *I have asked of the* LORD,
> *that <u>will I seek after</u>, inquire for and [insistently] require,*
> *that I may dwell in the house of the* LORD—*in his presence—all the*
> *days of my life,*
> *to behold and <u>gaze upon the sweet attractiveness</u>*
> *and <u>the delightful loveliness of the</u>* LORD,
> *and to meditate, consider and inquire in his temple.*
> *Psalm 27:4 (Amp)*
> (What is <u>your</u> 'one thing?)

> *You have said <u>seek my face</u>—*
> *inquire for and require my presence [as your vital need].*
> *My heart says to you,*
> *your face (your presence),* LORD, *will I seek,*
> *inquire for and [require of necessity and on the authority of your Word].*
> *Psalm 27:8 (Amp)*

David's undergirding desire in life was intimacy with God, and the verses above are only a small sample from many other similar ones. That's why he was a man after God's own heart, because he had a heart for God. That's what God is looking for above anything else in a man or woman.

When a person like that sins against God he is quick to repent, as we see in Psalm fifty one. And what was one thing that David dreaded because of his sin? Look at verse eleven:

> *Do not cast me from your presence*
> *or take your Holy Spirit from me.*

The enormous consequences of his sin had just struck David, and it wasn't about the loss of his kingship—it was the loss of intimacy with God.

## Paul—All else is rubbish

In 2 Corinthians 11 Paul lists some of the hardships he has faced in his Christian walk; beatings, lashings, shipwreck, starvation, prison, sleeplessness, starvation, betrayals, the burden of the churches, and more. What enables a man to go through all that? Here's the defining passage from Philippians 3, which explains it all, and we're looking at verses seven to eleven in J.B Phillips' translation.

> *… whatever was to my profit I now consider loss for the sake of Christ.*
> *What is more, I consider everything a loss compared to*
> *the surpassing greatness of knowing Christ Jesus my Lord,*
> *for whose sake I have lost all things. I consider them rubbish,*
> *that I may gain Christ*
> *and be found in him,*
> *not having a righteousness of my own that comes from the law,*
> *but that which is through faith in Christ—*
> *the righteousness that comes from God and is by faith.*
> *I want to know Christ and the power of his resurrection*

> *and the fellowship of sharing in his sufferings,*
> *becoming like him in his death,*
> *and so, somehow, to attain to the resurrection from the dead.*

And still Paul is not satisfied; he's longing for more of Jesus, as he explains in verses eleven to fourteen.

> *My brothers, I do not consider myself to have "arrived", spiritually,*
> *nor do I consider myself already perfect.*
> *But I keep going on, grasping ever more firmly that purpose for which*
> *Christ Jesus grasped me.*
> *My brothers, I do not consider myself to have fully grasped it even now.*
> *But I do concentrate on this:*
> *I leave the past behind*
> *and with hands outstretched to whatever lies ahead*
> *I go straight for the goal—*
> *my reward the honour of my high calling by God in Christ Jesus.*

Something had happened to Paul on that road to Damascus—and it wasn't conversion to a religion, or the Scriptures, or a system of belief. He had encountered Jesus in such a way that he could never rest until he had as much of him as it was possible to have this side of heaven. Through all his hard work and trials he never lost sight of this one undergirding, compelling, all-encompassing ambition—to know <u>Jesus</u>.

As regards the verb *to know* we have a problem in the English language, in that the word does not differentiate between knowing facts and knowing a person; or between knowing about a person and knowing them well. The Greek verb used in this passage is the equivalent, or so I'm told, of the Hebrew word in Genesis 4:1, where it says in the KJV, 'And Adam *knew* his wife; and she conceived…' That's more than just knowing <u>about</u> Eve, that's intimacy. However, we'll come back to that subject in a later chapter.

All these people were from bible days but as we go through the book we'll be looking at other people through the ages since the New Testament. We'll discover how their lives have been impacted by their passion for Jesus.

## Life without the presence of Jesus

What is the Christian life without the joy of Jesus' presence? It's little more than religion. The Christian life and church life can be such a drag without this close relationship with Jesus. It's how God's greatest workers were able to press through in the face of tremendous difficulties.

It's so easy to get caught up with working for Jesus and our work can often get in the way of fellowship with Jesus. That's not to say that service isn't essential but often we're too busy and too tired to deepen our fellowship with the Lord. Or maybe we just like working because it makes us feel we're doing something worthwhile.

There is a time and place for everything. For example, in any marriage there is a time for housework, going to the office or factory or other mundane activities. However, the wedding night isn't the time for such things. On the first night of the honeymoon the new husband doesn't expect his bride to don overalls and a cloth cap and start dusting the hotel bedroom. Nor will he be expected to put on a boiler suit or pull out his briefcase and catch up on some office work. That can come later, but just now there are more important things to do.

For many years I could make no headway with the Song of Solomon, then I read it in the Amplified Version which gave it new life for me. There are two or three ways, in general, of interpreting the Song of Solomon. In the Amplified Version the interpretation assumes that King Solomon has become decadent by this time, having been drawn away from his wholehearted pursuit of God by his many wives concubines, riches etc. A young girl wanders by accident into King Solomon's gardens and, as she is very beautiful, she is taken, against her will, into Solomon's harem. The book is a tussle between her resisting the wooing by Solomon and her loyalty to her lover, the shepherd from her home village.

It's a picture of the church and Jesus; how she is so often seduced away from her Lord, who is always seeking to win her back.

In chapter five we find the girl longing for her lover, the shepherd, (verses two to six). As she is sleeping she hears him at the door.

*"Open to me, my sister, my darling, my dove, my flawless one."*

You would have thought that she would have leapt out of bed to let him in but, as she says, "I have taken off my robe—must I put it on again? I have washed my feet—must I soil them again?" He puts his hand through the hole in the door to try to reach the latch and, as she hears this, at last the girl leaps out of bed to let him in. But she's too late, he's gone. She's missed him. All that's left is the scent of his presence which he has left behind.

*"I arose to open for my lover, and my hands dripped with myrrh,*
*on the handles of the lock. I opened for my lover,*
*but my lover had left; he was gone.*
*My heart sank at his departure."*

How often have we missed real intimacy with Jesus and been left with only the mere scent of his presence because we have been too slow to respond? How often have we just continued to sing songs and missed real worship because of our lack of responsiveness? Oh, how we need to develop in our sensitivity to the gentle leadings of the Holy Spirit.

## Love letter to Ephesus

The importance to God of our relationship to him is emphasised in the letter to the church in Ephesus recorded in Revelation chapter two. What a good church that was according to our Western way of making assessments. Working hard and persevering, doctrinally pure and still not wearied after persecution. I wonder what the leader of the church thought as he read the first few lines of the letter." We've got to be in the running for a reward here, folks, the Lord likes us". He must have got a real shock, though, as he read on, It wasn't just that the Lord said he had something against them, it was the strength of his disapproval. And what was their misdemeanour? It certainly wasn't any of the sins we might normally think about like money, sex or power. What he said was simply this:

*"You have forsaken your first love. Remember the height from which you have fallen."*

That's all; they were not as passionately in love with Jesus as they had been initially. They had lost that intimate relationship with him and that's what he desires above all else. It was a cry that came right from his heart. "We've lost something vital; I'd rather have your passionate love than all these other good things put together." It's interesting to note that the only two of the seven churches to receive an out-and-out corporate rebuke were those in Ephesus and Laodicea. One had lost its first love and one was lukewarm.

## A call to greater intimacy

I believe that the strongest call of the Father and of Jesus in these days is that of drawing closer in our relationship, both individually and corporately as a church. Let's respond to that call wholeheartedly—our own future and that of the world depends very much on how well we answer that call.

# CHAPTER 3

# Intimacy of Sonship

## A new understanding for me

Some time ago I was reading through Galatians and I was struck by a verse in chapter three, verse fourteen.

*He redeemed us in order that the blessing given to Abraham*
*might come to the Gentiles through Christ Jesus,*
*so that by faith we might receive the promise of the Spirit.*

We're all familiar with the expression, 'the bottom line', which means this is where it's at, this is the aim of the whole exercise etc. It was the bottom line in this verse that really struck me, and in fact it is the last line of the verse. What Paul seems to be saying here is that the bottom line of God's plan for us is that we should receive the Holy Spirit, but I had always considered that God's bottom line for us is salvation. Now I know that the baptism in the Holy Spirit is extremely important, as is the equipping of the Holy Spirit, but I couldn't reconcile these two aspects with this 'bottom line'.

It wasn't until three or four years later that I got my answer. Once again I was reading through Galatians when I was struck by chapter four, verse six, which says,

> *Because you are sons, God sent the Spirit of his Son into our hearts,*
> *the Spirit who calls out, "Abba, Father."*

It was the phrase, 'God sent the Spirit of his Son into our hearts that turned on all the lights for me. Although Paul is clearly referring to the Holy Spirit here, he doesn't refer to him in that way; he calls him the Spirit of his, that is God's, Son. In other words we're talking here about our adoption as God's sons, but not just in a theological way, but as an intimate relationship. In looking further into this we need to go back in time, to the creation of man.

## Bridging the understanding gap

One of the 'problems' that God has is revealing the truth about himself to mankind. The basic problem is that God is 'altogether other' than us. He is eternal, Spirit, infinite, and conveying knowledge about himself to us, who are bound up in this limited space/time dimension, is difficult. We're a bit like goldfish in a bowl that, at best, can see no farther than the walls of the room where its bowl is kept. In the same way our ability to understand God, who is Spirit, is so limited. So God has to express himself in concepts which we can understand, and one of those concepts is the relationship of fatherhood. Another is the marriage relationship, which we'll look at in the next chapter. I believe that God's purpose with both these relationships is primarily as 'mega' parables to reveal himself to us.

Please note that when I talk about *sons* this is not gender specific; we know that 'there is neither male nor female' in God's family. However, in looking at this concept in its totality, we would lose some of its significance if we brought in the term *daughter*. This is because in Jesus' day sons and daughters didn't have the same rights and privileges, although in God's kingdom both sexes have exactly the same.

One of God's greatest urges within himself is fatherhood. It is God's desire to produce after his own kind—so he made Adam in his own image. Obviously Adam was limited, nevertheless he inherited God's own nature. When God breathed into Adam, not only did he confer life, but also his own genetic code through the Holy Spirit. Adam didn't have just human life but he was a son of God. God had put within him his own seed. God was just as pleased, no even more so, than any human father with his newly acquired son, and they spent many a long hour together having fellowship, intimate communication, in the Garden of Eden.

We all know that that relationship was broken by sin, Adam's disobedience. When that happened God lost a son, he was literally bereaved, which was expressed in God's cry of, "Adam, where are you?" He knew where Adam was physically (God is omnipresent, after all), but it was a cry of anguish, a deep groan of mourning. God had watched his son, created in his own image, die spiritually. That's why we're told that we are 'dead in trespasses and sins'. The relationship with our true Father has been severed as completely and abruptly as death separates us in the physical realm.

But God, the Father, wants and longs for that relationship back again. God hadn't made man because he wanted a gardener or a zoo keeper, but because he wanted an intimate father/son relationship. I'm sure that when Jesus told the parable of the Prodigal Son he felt the pathos of it so very keenly. He knew how his own Father, our Father, felt about the loss of his human sons, so this parable was, I'm sure, especially poignant for Jesus to tell. Fathers want sons, that's what makes them fathers, and God wanted his sons back again.

This is expressed in Ephesians 3:15 (JBP) in this way:

*... I fall on my knees before the Father*
*(from whom all fatherhood, earthly or heavenly, derives its name) ...*

We are seeing today the tragedy of a fatherless generation. It's a generation where a high percentage of sons have only biological fathers. They have never known the presence of their father, never known the intimacy of a father/son relationship, never had a father as a real role model. And of those who have only biological fathers, many have been conceived by artificial insemination by donor, and may never know who provided the semen. How very different to the way the Father intended it to be.

## Jesus & Abba

God the Father has always longed for this relationship with man to be restored, so he sent Jesus, his Son, to earth. Jesus not only came to die for our sins, but I believe he also came to role model the father/son relationship. Time and time again in the gospels we see the evidence of the intimate relationship Jesus had with his Father, and it was there at the public launching of his ministry. Let's look at the baptism scene on the banks of the River Jordan.

*As Jesus was coming up out of the water,*
*he saw heaven being torn open*
*and the Spirit descending on him like a dove.*
*And a voice came from heaven:*
*"You are my <u>Son</u>, whom I love; with you I am well pleased."*
Mark 1:10

Here we see all three members of the Trinity in action together, all working within their own functions. At this point Jesus was equipped with power from the Holy Spirit, but I wonder if something else was happening there at the same time. As the Father declared Jesus to be his own, well-loved Son, did something take place within the spirit of Jesus? Did the Holy Spirit convey to

Jesus at this point a new realisation of the reality of his sonship? Jesus knew already who he was, as evidenced when he was twelve years old, conversing with the religious leaders in the Temple at Jerusalem ("... don't you know I must be about my Father's business?" Luke 2:49), but did the realisation go to a new depth at this stage?

Let's go now to the last part of Jesus' ministry, when he was on the cross. He cried out, "My God, my God why have you forsaken me?", and it's how he addressed God that made me think. Previously he'd said, "Father, forgive them ...", then later, "Father, into your hands I commit our spirits." Could it be that the agony of being forsaken was that his Father had withdrawn the Holy Spirit, the Spirit of Sonship, at this point? Now he only knew in his head that he was God's son. The intimacy of sonship had been lost. He *knew* finally the greatest agony of a fallen creation, a creation without a father. That was the blackness. He no longer felt a sense of belonging, his Father was 'gone'. He knew the agony of being without the Spirit who made him a son. He now felt like an 'orphan', the way mankind is before redemption.

That experience of Jesus is one of the reasons he can identify with those of us who have no fathers, or don't know who they are. To have had something and then lost it can often feel worse than never having had it in the first place. Jesus had had that intimacy with his Father, but now it was gone. Yes, Jesus felt the pain of being fatherless at that point in time, just when he needed his Father's presence most.

Is that why David begged God in Psalm fifty one not to take away his Spirit from him? The thought of losing the *felt* sense of sonship was too painful to bear.

The purpose of Jesus on earth was to bring mankind back to the Father heart of God. The great desire of Father God is to restore relationship with his children, so Jesus came to reveal the Father. And it was God as the *Father* he came to reveal. A very well-known passage from John chapter fourteen (verses six to nine) illustrates this very clearly.

*Jesus answered, "I am the way and the truth and the life.*
*No-one comes to the Father except through me.*
*If you really knew me, you would know my Father as well.*
*From now on, you do know him and have seen him."*
*Philip said, "Lord, show us the Father and that will be enough for us."*
*Jesus answered: "Don't you know me, Philip, even after I have been*
*among you such a long time?*
*Anyone who has seen me has seen the Father.*
*How can you say, 'Show us the Father'?"*

God could easily have demonstrated his 'Godness' by doing spectacular acts and shows of authority and power. But to reveal his Fatherhood he needed to demonstrate it through his Son. Jesus spent much time alone with his Father, and he only ever said what his Father told him to say, and only did what he saw his Father do. What a picture of sonship; what a picture of role modelling. Here are just three of the references Jesus made explaining how he related to his Father's work.

*I am telling you what I have seen in the Father's presence.*
*John 8:38.*

*The world must learn that I love the Father*
*and that I do exactly what my Father has commanded me.*
*John 14:31*

*Don't you believe that I am in the Father, and that the Father is in me?*
*The words I say to you are not just my own.*
*Rather, it is the Father, living in me, who is doing his work.*
*John 14:10*

I don't know of any other religion where God is portrayed in such a clear way as our Father, and where he wants such an intimate relationship.

## Us & Abba

We've just seen how Jesus asked the disciples this question, "If you really knew me, you would know my Father as well." (John 14:7), which brings me to the question, how well do you know the *Father*, not *God*, but the *Father*? Have you entered yet into the full revelation of sonship? How well entwined is the Holy Spirit with yours, assuring you that God really is your Father? What is your main perception of your relationship to God? Does it *feel* like a good father/son relationship? Many Christians still know God only as God, and many have a growing intimate relationship with Jesus, but how many are growing in that secure, intimate knowledge of the Father?

During the period of three months when all this revelation was coming to me I was very sharply focused on my relationship with the Father. I realised at one point that, in a sense, I seemed to be 'ignoring' Jesus. Now that was odd for me because for many years I'd been pursuing the goal of intimacy with Jesus. In fact I said to him one day, "I seem to be ignoring you at the moment, Jesus, and just concentrating on the Father. Is that alright?" And I sensed him reply, "That's alright because that's what I came for ultimately, to reveal the Father and show people the way back to *him*." It seems to me now that if we stick at knowing Jesus (which is tremendous in itself), we've not completed the course.

We've not 'arrived' until we finish up in the Father's embrace, in an intimate Father/son relationship with him. We don't have time to go into that aspect in further detail just now, but I find it to be a fascinating concept.

For many of us a great stumbling block to developing a relationship with Father God has been the relationship (or lack of it) with our natural father. If we've not had that kind of relationship with our earthly father it can be very difficult to grow into a deep relationship with our heavenly Father. If our natural father has been absent or cruel then the difficulty can be huge.

Many fathers have been good in respect of providing for their families and giving security, but without expressing their tender love adequately. This makes for sons who respect their fathers, but don't have an intimate relationship with them. What we're looking at here is not so much a God who is looking for respect, but a Father who is looking for intimacy, a Father who has demonstrated his love for us by sending Jesus to give his life for us. And not only that, because the dying of Jesus on the cross was only the start, it's the initiation into a relationship that ought to keep on going deeper forever. And it's more than knowing about—it's about experiencing.

The big question is, however, how do we develop this relationship? For those of us who have had less than adequate relationships with our natural fathers there is an extra degree of difficulty in this process.

Let's look again at Galatians 4:6.

*Because you are sons, <u>God **sent** the Spirit of his Son into our hearts,</u>*
*<u>the Spirit who calls out, "Abba, Father."</u>*
*So you are no longer a slave, but a son;*
*and since you are a son, God has made you also an heir.*

And then at Romans 8:14-16,

*Those who are led by the Spirit of God are sons of God.*
*For you did not receive a spirit that makes you a slave again to fear,*

> *but you **received** the Spirit of sonship.*
> *And by him we cry, "Abba, Father."*

The Greek word for *call out* in Galatians 4:6 is same as when Jesus cried out on the cross, "My God, my God, why have you forgotten me?" It's a cry of deep feeling and emotion coming from a person's innermost being. In Galatians 4:6 it's a different kind of emotion, of course, one of joy in this case.

It's important to note how this calling out works. In Galatians it's the Spirit who calls out, whereas in Romans it's we who cry out by the Spirit. I don't know how it works and the only way I can picture it is that Holy Spirit entwines himself round my spirit, and together we call out, "Abba, Father."

This is something generated by the Spirit, not by us, we're just carried along by him. Interestingly enough, the Good News Translation says that 'God's Spirit <u>joins himself</u> to our spirits to declare that we are God's children.'

This throws the whole issue back to the Holy Spirit; it's his job to bring us into this place of Father/son intimacy; it's not something we have to strive for, we just need to receive from the Spirit. 'God sent … you received', is how these two passages link together.

Salvation is much more than 'believe on the Lord Jesus Christ and you will be saved'. That will do for starters, but there's a much greater richness than that. It's about the Spirit of sonship, about *felt* love, and everything that goes with it, such as,

- Love
- Belonging
- Security
- Intimacy
- Strength

27

All this goes far beyond mere head knowledge. In fact, when the Holy Spirit is engaging with our spirits at a very deep level, often the mind doesn't understand what's happening. There is a level of communication in the Spirit where there is edification going on in the inner man but in which the brain has no part. Nevertheless there is a definite transaction occurring which is very beneficial.

As I was discussing this point with a friend of mine one time he made the following comment, "I'm understanding something in my spirit just now, but my mind has no understanding of it at all." When the Holy Spirit communicates *Abba* to us at this level there is a sense of joy and fulfilment which cannot be described. And it can happen in the most adverse of circumstances.

This is same Spirit that Jesus had—the Spirit of sonship and it is a place of deep intimacy. It's something we *receive* from God and it comes only by revelation. However, it's not something reserved just for an élite few, it's open to all who really want to pursue the goal of intimacy.

Of course, this description of the crying out in the Spirit is one of worship. It has a different feel to that of a bride and groom of course. Here we're talking about the closeness of a father and his son. And the worship that the son gives his father is one born out of love, dependency, trust, respect, awe etc. And the father accepts it, not in an egotistical way, but in a tender, loving way. It's not the worship that the Father values most of all, it's the worshipper, the closeness of his son.

Without doubt, our Father is an awesome God, beyond the power of words to describe, beyond human intellect even to begin to understand, but the essence of true worship is not solely with God's greatness, but with his Father heart. The Father is seeking worshippers (John 4:23).

Mankind has so often misrepresented God because it has not understood the *Fatherhood* of God. There are a couple of phrases in John 8:54–55 which I find very striking:

*Jesus replied, "If I glorify myself, my glory means nothing.*
*My Father, whom you claim as your God, is the one who glorifies me.*
*Though you do not know him, I know him.*
*If I said I did not, I would be a liar like you,*
*but I do know him and keep his word.*

"My Father, whom you claim as your God ... you do not know him ..." That phrase speaks volumes to me. We claim the Father as our God, yet we know so little of his Father heart, so we grossly misrepresent him. We portray him either as a holy but unyielding, judgemental God, or as a 'sugar daddy', more often the former being our model. When we miss God's Father heart. then we miss the essence of what salvation is about—restoring the intimacy of the Father/son relationship. How badly the religious leaders of Jesus' day missed it, and how badly we so often miss it today.

I think that Islam is a case in point, where God (Allah) is portrayed in his greatness, but where his Fatherhood is not understood. This is, in fact, the essence of Bilquis Sheikh's book, *I Dared to Call Him Father*, where she describes how her journey from Islam to Christianity was energised as God revealed himself to her as her *Father.*

In her book Mrs Sheikh describes how she was reading both the Koran and the bible, trying to decide which one was really God's word. Here's an extract where she tells of her great discovery.

"I am confused, Father," I said. "I have to get one thing straight right away." I reached over to the bedside table where I kept the Bible and the Koran side by side.

I picked up both books and lifted them, one in each hand. "Which, Father?" I said. "Which one is Your book?"

Then a remarkable thing happened. Nothing like it had ever occurred in my life in quite this way. For I heard a voice inside my being, a voice that spoke to me as clearly as if I were repeating words in my inner mind. They were fresh, full of kindness, yet at the same time full of authority.

"In which book do you meet Me as your Father?" I found myself answering: "In the Bible."

That's all it took. Now there was no question in my mind which one was His book. I looked at my watch and was astonished to discover that three hours had passed. Yet I was not tired. I wanted to go on praying, I wanted to read the Bible, for I knew now that my Father would speak through it. I went to bed only when I knew I must for the sake of my health. But the very next morning I told my maids to see that I was not disturbed, took my Bible again and reclined on my divan. Starting with Matthew, I began reading the New Testament word by word.

John 16:2-3 has something interesting to say along these lines:

> *They will put you out of the synagogue; in fact,*
> *a time is coming when anyone who kills you*
> *will think he is offering a service to God.*
> *They will do such things because <u>they have not known the **Father**</u> or me.*

How often have Christians mistreated and persecuted *one another* because we have not really known the *Father*. We've not really experienced his Father heart. If we had his heart we wouldn't ill-treat our brothers and sisters, even if they don't see things exactly the way we do. We've also pursued nonbelievers out of a zeal for 'truth' rather than being motivated by the love of our Father, and that's caused all kinds of problems. We Christians have got it wrong so often for this very reason, we've pursued so-called truth, but without reflecting the Father's heart.

1 Corinthians 13 expresses the same principle in a different way—if we don't have love, nothing we do is of any value, and of course God, our Father, *is* love. I know that, in recent times, I've had to search my own heart in relation to the many things I've said and done 'in God's name' without echoing his Father heart. I can tell you that I've done a lot of cringing!

So the big question is, how well do we know God as our Father? How deeply is the Spirit crying through us, "Abba, Father"? Are we *aware* of this, are our emotions involved? Is it something we're growing in steadily? This knowing the Father intimately is the key to the quality and effectiveness of our lives. If we don't *know,* if we don't feel in our spirits that we're sons, then we feel like orphans and produce symptoms such as these.

- We strive for the praise, approval, and acceptance of man instead of feeling totally accepted in God's love and justified by grace.
- As far as service is concerned, we sense a need for personal achievement as we seek to impress God and others. On the other hand we have no motivation to serve at all, instead of giving service that is motivated by a deep gratitude for being unconditionally loved and accepted by God
- When thinking about our position in God we feel like a servant or slave, rather than feeling like a son or daughter
- When we look at other Christians we do so on the basis of competition, rivalry, and jealousy towards their success

and position. Those who *feel* like sons have humility and unity as they value others and are able to rejoice in their blessings and success

Do you remember when Jesus talked about receiving the kingdom of God as a child? I wonder if what he had in mind was the simple security of childlike trust in a father's love. This is a place where it's not so much matter of grasping objective truth, but of lying back peacefully in our Heavenly Father's embrace.

I've said that our emotions should be involved, and that's true; however, the acid test is not about how we feel, but on the fruit we produce. 1 John 2:3-6 puts it very clearly:

*We know that we have come to know him if we obey his commands.*
*The man who says, "I know him," but does not do what he commands*
*is a liar, and the truth is not in him.*
*But if anyone obeys his word,*
*God's love is truly made complete in him.*
*This is how we know we are in him:*
*Whoever claims to live in him must walk as Jesus did.*

When we are born into a natural family we carry the characteristics of our parents. We take on these characteristics, however, in two different ways; some we inherit genetically, for example our colouring, intelligence, predisposition to certain illnesses, build etc. Others we receive by absorption, the effect of being with people from our earliest existence. These would include, amongst other things, the way we act, our life values, our cultural inheritance. A child adopted soon after birth will only show the genetically inherited characteristics of its biological parents, but the main influence on the kind of adult it grows up to be will be what it learns and absorbs from its adoptive parents.

In the same way, when we are born again into God's family there are certain things that we inherit simply by that birth process, like eternal life, our general direction. On the other hand there are many aspects that we take on only by being in the company of our Heavenly Father. It's as we get to know him that we are moulded by him and continuously reflect more and more of his characteristics and personality. If we are not growing in intimacy then we're not growing in his likeness. We're not showing the fruit which Jesus said is the proof of our living in him, or which John echoed in the passage we've just quoted.

The big question is, am I more like my heavenly Father now than I was last year? That's the measure of my growing intimacy. And that's where we should be heading according to Romans 8:29

*For those God foreknew*
*He also predestined to be conformed to the likeness of his Son,*
*That he might be the firstborn among many brothers.*

Just a thought at the end of this section; does the nature (as well as the degree) of our intimacy with our Father change as we mature? After all, the intimacy of a father with his three month old baby son is greatly different in its form and expression from that for his thirty year old son. At an older age communication is so different, but also so much more two-way. Although the father/son relationship is, and always will be, there, it's now more of a relationship of equals.

As I understand it, although *abba* is a term of intimacy it's not equivalent to our *daddy*. It carries with it more of a mature sense. A fully mature son in Jesus' day would have called his father "Abba," which would have carried with it a sense both of intimacy and respect.

# CHAPTER 4

# Bridal Intimacy

As I mentioned in the last chapter, I believe that there are two great life parables which God has given to humankind, that of marriage and that of fatherhood. When you're a spirit, as God is, and infinite, it is very difficult to communicate who you really are to human beings who are so restricted in a space/time existence. That applies even though we were made in God's own image. So God has chosen to speak to us through parables, which in this case are not spoken parables, but what I call *life parables*.

The Scripture which expresses this thought succinctly is Ephesians 5:32, which is part of Paul's discourse on how married couples should relate to one other.

*This is a profound mystery—*
*but I am talking about Christ and the church.*

When the Godhead wanted to describe the relationship of Jesus to the church (at that time a future event) marriage is what was decided upon. Primarily this is what marriage is about, not propagation of the species or about a good way of raising children; these aspects are part of the package but not the bottom line. I believe that marriage is primarily about intimacy and all that it brings with it as a demonstration of Jesus' intimacy with his bride, the church.

This is why Christian marriage is so important, because we are saying to the world, "Look at our marriage, it's a parable about the love of Jesus for his church, and his relationship to her." That, of course, should make us Christians think very seriously about the implications of divorce. I'm not saying that there aren't circumstances where this might be necessary, but it's worrying when divorce rates among Christians are as high as they are with those who aren't.

We often use the image of bridal intimacy to illustrate our relationship as individuals to the Lord; however, whilst lessons drawn may be true, I don't believe that this is the proper interpretation of bridal intimacy. As far as I can see this parable is used only of corporate relationship to the Lord, in other words, Israel in the Old Testament and the church in the New Testament.

Even before the era of the church God used this parable in relation to his chosen nation Israel. When she was unfaithful to him, unfortunately all too often, he frequently described this unfaithfulness as adultery.

God spoke to Israel very forcefully, even shockingly, through the prophet Hosea, during one of these periods of unfaithfulness. Listen to his instruction to Hosea (Hosea 1:2).

*When the LORD began to speak through Hosea, the LORD said to him, "Go, take to yourself an adulterous wife and children of unfaithfulness, because the land is guilty of the vilest adultery in departing from the LORD."*

One aspect of this scenario that really strikes me is that God was prepared to break his own rules in order to make his point, so he must have felt very strongly about it. God goes on to say how he will punish Israel because of her spiritual adultery, then he brings in a very tender note in Hosea 2:14:

*"Therefore I am now going to allure her;*
*I will lead her into the desert and speak tenderly to her."*

In Jeremiah 2:2 we have the same theme again:

*"Go and proclaim in the hearing of Jerusalem:*
*'I remember the devotion of your youth,*
*how as a bride you loved me and followed me through the desert,*
*through a land not sown.'"*

And so this theme runs throughout the Old Testament, and the one thing it illustrates is that what God is primarily looking for is relationship, love. Whilst it's true that he is a holy God and we must always have that aspect of him firmly in our sights, his primary aim is not to have us obeying a set of rules. He is after our hearts. Just prior to entering the Promised land God gave Moses a new commandment. It was one that was striking in its simplicity, especially for the Old Testament. In Deuteronomy 6:5 Moses is simply told:

*Love the* LORD *your God*
*with all your heart*
*and with all your soul*
*and with all your strength.*

That's quite a contrast to the Ten Commandments and all the other long list of instructions in the books of Moses. I think it's significant in its timing, too, just as the Israelites were about to enter a new dimension of living.

God said the same thing in Hosea 6:6 (Today's English Version):

*"I want your constant love, not your animal sacrifices."*

I've already touched on Song of Solomon. Although there has been much discussion in the past on whether this book should even be in the bible, it portrays so graphically this whole theme of bridal intimacy. It also describes vividly how strong the temptation is to be drawn away from one's true love.

Solomon tried his hardest to woo the young woman away from her shepherd lover, and it would have been so easy for her to succumb to his charms and great wealth. Even though she faltered on an occasion (5:2-8), in the end she remained totally faithful. Reading this book through in the Amplified Version certainly showed to me in a new way how strong is the passion of Jesus for his church, and how desirable it is for her to reciprocate.

When thinking about how Jesus loves and wants to relate to his church, just let your imagination run wild with Song of Solomon. Let it capture your heart, then skip to the very end of the bible, to the last few chapters of Revelation. We've already seen where John's passion lay—for intimacy with his Lord and his Heavenly Father, so when he wrote the following verses, I'm sure he was thrilled to do so. In Revelation 19:7 and 9 he writes:

> *Let us rejoice and be glad and give him glory!*
> *For the wedding of the Lamb has come,*
> *and his bride has made herself ready.*
> *Then the angel said to me,*
> *"Write: 'Blessed are those who are invited*
> *to the wedding supper of the Lamb!'"*

This is the culmination of the ages, the ushering in of something completely new, the completion of our salvation and commencement of eternal life. And God says it's like a wedding feast. This is what Jesus has been longing for, this is the result of his agony on the cross, this is what he died for—union with his bride, the church. Then in chapter twenty one, verse two John writes this:

> *I saw the Holy City, the new Jerusalem,*
> *coming down out of heaven from God,*
> *prepared as a bride*
> *beautifully dressed for her husband.*

Then it seems like the excitement and glory of it all has John mixing up his metaphors, as we see in verses nine to eleven of this chapter:

> *One of the seven angels who had the seven bowls full of the*
> *seven last plagues came and said to me,*
> *"Come, I will show you the bride, the wife of the Lamb."*
> *And he carried me away in the Spirit to a mountain great and high,*
> *and showed me the Holy City, Jerusalem,*
> *coming down out of heaven from God.*
> *It shone with the glory of God,*
> *and its brilliance was like that of a very precious jewel,*
> *like a jasper, clear as crystal.*

This is the ultimate destination of the church, union with her Bridegroom, Jesus Christ. This bride had taken time and trouble to get herself ready; it's not been a rushed, last minute affair. And as in any relationship of this kind, there has been a gradual increase of intimacy as time has passed. There's been an increasing desire for the final intimacy. Unfortunately, in these modern times, much of the significance of this has been missed because we're now in an age of instant gratification and pleasure without commitment.

I wonder if the church is really preparing herself as she ought to be? Will the final change have to be massive because we've taken so little time to prepare ourselves? Are we becoming purer day by day, is intimacy increasing, are we really longing for greater union with Jesus? Or does the world attract us too much, or, on the other hand, are we so busy working for Jesus with a servant mentality that we've never taken the time to deepen our relationship?

There is an insistent call to us to get ready, as Revelation 22:17 says:

> *The Spirit and the bride say, "Come!"*
> *And let him who hears say, "Come!"*
> *Whoever is thirsty, let him come;*
> *and whoever wishes,*
> *let him take the free gift of the water of life.*

Jesus even used the illustration of getting ready for a wedding on more than one occasion in connection with his second coming.

I mentioned earlier that incident in Song of Solomon (2:5–6) where the young woman can't be bothered getting out of bed when she hears her lover at the door. What an incomprehensible tragedy—she's longing for him so passionately, yet when he calls she can't be bothered. But isn't that what happened with the church in Laodicea (Revelation chapter three)?

> *Here I am!*
> *I stand at the door and knock.*
> *If anyone one hears ….*

How often does this happen with churches today? We're so often too busy with our own plans, programmes and busyness. We're too tired to get up because of it all—and Jesus stands there still—knocking, knocking, knocking. Are we crazy or something?

39

This is not meant to be a comprehensive study on the Bride of Christ, we're just taking one aspect of this parable to illustrate the subject of this book: intimacy. Marital intimacy is the closest union you can get in human terms, and God designed marriage to show us how close he wants the relationship of the church and Jesus to be. Surely we can understand from this that it's all about relationship, about restoring a relationship that God always wanted.

Basilea Schlink in *Bridal Love* puts it this way:

> Jesus, who so often says "Whoever loves Me," ... "Do you love Me?" is concerned about our LOVE!

> He is concerned about a special kind of love. It is the love which is shadowed in the relationship between a bride and her bridegroom; that is, it is an exclusive love, a love which places the beloved, the bridegroom, above all other loves, in the first place. As a Bridegroom, Jesus has a claim to "first love". He who has loved us so much wants to possess us completely, with everything we are and have. Jesus gave Himself wholly and completely for us. Now His love is yearning for us to surrender ourselves and everything that we are to Him, so that He can really be our "first love".

> So long as our love for Him is a divided love, so long as our heart is bound to family, possessions, or the like, He will not count our love to be genuine. Divided love is of so little value to Him that He will not enter into a bond of love with such a soul, for this bond presupposes a full mutual

love. Because our love is so precious to Jesus, because He yearns for our love, He waits for our uncompromising commitment.

When John was told to write to the church in Ephesus (as we saw in chapter one) the Lord's problem with her was that she had lost her first love. That can mean equally well that she didn't love as she did at first, or that the Lord was no longer the first love of her life. Yet the church wasn't a bad church; we're not told that she was worldly or that there was rampant sin in the place. She just wasn't as passionately in love with Jesus as she had been or could be.

Maybe her idolatry was in her programmes, her works, her achievements etc. Maybe it was from these things she derived joy and satisfaction. I heard a good definition of idolatry recently:

> "Idolatry is when anything else but Jesus
> satisfies our deepest longings."

I like that, but find it very challenging.

In the latter half of the 1990s, with the Toronto Airport Christian Fellowship as its epicentre, there was a powerful move of the Holy Spirit. Some of its characteristics were laughter, weeping, strange noises and actions etc. Then, after a while, many churches that experienced these things began to quieten down again, reverting to 'normal' eventually. People have asked, "What was it all about, then? After all, it seemed so genuine at the time." I believe that God was doing many things at that time, but I think that one of the things that Jesus was doing was wooing the church. He certainly was changing individuals, but I think that there was a very corporate aim in what he was doing.

I've already referred to that passage in Hosea which refers to God's alluring of his unfaithful bride, Israel. I think that was what was happening with much of the weird-looking stuff associated with Toronto and other places.

One of the characteristics of young, fresh love is the absence of dignity, and often utter nonsense is talked, which, in any other context would seem crazy. It's just that the two lovers are so overwhelmed with one another that rationality goes out of the window, and all that matters is that they are together and communicating. In the same way I believe that Jesus was wooing his bride, and in so doing he had to break down that stiff, cerebral attitude which we in the West have had for so long in relationship to our spirituality. I don't mean, of course, that we have to throw out our brains, but we do need to grow into a real heart relationship with the Lord.

We all know that one of the worst thing that can happen to a wooer is that the object of his love doesn't respond in kind. Many men have committed suicide for that very reason. So one of the expectations of Jesus is that, having been wooed by him, his bride, the church, should now respond proportionately. In other words, it's now our turn to seek his face diligently. Maybe the reason so many churches who enjoyed the Lord's presence so much a few years ago, but who are now 'flat' again is that they haven't pursued this intimacy with Jesus, they haven't followed hard after him.

I heard Tommy Tenney illustrate this point by telling about his daughter and himself. He describes how sometimes his young daughter would chase her dad round the garden, which Tommy would do, intentionally keeping just ahead of her. Eventually, because he wanted to embrace her, he would stop, turn round and throw his arms around her. He said, "We chase God until he turns round and catches us." The tragedy is that we just don't chase after him as we ought to.

In our private lives we chase after money, security, comfort, recognition, pleasure etc. In our church lives we chase after growth, comfortable premises, plans, programmes, recognition and so many other things, but not his pure presence. And because we don't eagerly and persistently pursue him he doesn't turn round and catch us. What a tragedy!

And, at the end of the day, fruitfulness comes from intimacy. Why is it that we understand this in the natural, but don't seem to be able to grasp it in the spiritual realm? Even when so much of our church works are so sterile we often don't seem to be able to wake up to the fact of this principle.

So what are we meant to learn from all this? Several things.

- Jesus doesn't desire intimacy from us only as individuals, but also as a corporate body.
- He wants the church passionately to be in love with him and he desires this above anything else. In fact he will go to great lengths to bring us to this point.
- The exclusivity of his love for us—and his desire for the same from us. There's no room for competitors. Jesus' commitment to his bride is total, and our relationship with him should be the same.
- Even when we're cool towards him his love is always hot towards us.
- Total intimacy is the final destination of the church.

# CHAPTER 5

# The Intimacy of Shared Life

For me, what John writes in chapters fourteen, fifteen and sixteen of his gospel summarises the very kernel of what our salvation is about. He was a man for whom intimacy with his Lord was his prime concern. I'm sure he would identify with Paul's statement in Philippians 3:10. "That I may know Christ ..." We find him reclining with his head on Jesus' chest during the last supper, and something like fifty years later when he wrote his first letter, he is still fascinated with this close fellowship with Jesus. This is what he wrote in the first three verses of the letter, as translated by J.B. Phillips:

*We are writing to you about something which has always existed,*
*yet which we ourselves actually heard and saw with our own eyes:*
*something which we had opportunity to observe closely*
*and even to hold in our hands,*
*something of the Word of life!*
*For it was life which appeared before us:*
*we saw it, we are eyewitnesses of it,*
*and are now writing to you about it.*
*It was the very life of all ages,*
*the life that has always existed with the Father,*
*which actually became visible in person to us.*

*We repeat, we really saw and heard*
*what we are now writing to you about.*
*We want you to be with us in this—*
*in this fellowship with the Father, and Jesus Christ his Son.*

Kenneth Wuest translates verse one in an interesting way, one which catches clearly how John is feeling as he writes his letter:

*That which was from the beginning, that which we have heard,*
*with the present result that <u>it is ringing in our ears</u>.*

Don't you think there's an excitement coming from John as he writes these words—"we heard and saw with our own eyes—even to hold in our hands." The man's positively bubbling over with the sheer thrill of *knowing* Jesus, something that the passage of fifty years hasn't dulled in the least. What he reports Jesus saying in those three chapters of his gospel gives a clue as to why he writes the way he does in his first letter.

You'll be well aware that this discourse by Jesus takes place during and immediately after the last supper. Chapter fifteen records the events just after Judas had left to betray him. Therefore, what Jesus has to say carries immense weight, as you would expect.

## Father and Son—and Us

One of the things that stands out in this discourse is the intimacy between Father, Son and Holy Spirit. Let's start off with chapter fourteen, verses ten and eleven:

*"Don't you believe that <u>I am in the Father,</u>*
*and that <u>the Father is in me</u>?*
*The words I say to you are not just my own.*

*Rather, it is the Father, living in me, who is doing his work.*
*Believe me when I say that I am in the Father and the Father is in me;*
*or at least believe on the evidence of the miracles themselves."*

It doesn't take much explaining to see how closely Jesus and his Father were relating. There is a total merging of personalities. Then Jesus goes on to bring in the Holy Spirit and us, in verses sixteen and seventeen:

*"I will ask the Father, and he will give you another Counsellor to be*
*with you for ever—the Spirit of truth.*
*The world cannot accept him,*
*because it neither sees him nor knows him.*
*But you know him, for <u>he lives with you and will be in you</u>."*

So what we have here is the same kind of relationship, but involving Holy Spirit and us. Jesus goes on to say that, although he's going away, he's coming back again (verse eighteen). He's not referring, however, to the 'second coming' (*parousia*), but *to the Holy* Spirit. Then he goes on to say something totally mind blowing in verse twenty, referring to the coming of the Spirit:

*"On that day you will realise that I am in my Father,*
*and you are in me, and I am in you."*

Now I don't know about you, but this begins to trip out my tiny little mind on overload. The thought of this intimately-related-and-operating Trinity then coming to live in me just beggars the imagination; but that's what Jesus said. And just in case you wondered if you'd heard right Jesus emphasises this whole concept in verse twenty three.

*"If any one loves me, he will obey my teaching.*
*My Father will love him,*
*and we will come to him and make our home with him."*

## Enter the Holy Spirit

Now, still reeling from the shock of all this stuff, we'll skip over to chapter sixteen. Here we have a crowd of young men trying to take in two main ideas. The first one is that Jesus is going to leave them alone after three and a half years of sharing his life with them. The second one comes when Jesus makes this incredible statement to them in verse seven:

*"But I tell you the truth: It is for your good that I am going away.*
*Unless I go away, the Counsellor will not come to you;*
*but if I go, I will send him to you."*

You can understand these earliest of disciples struggling with what Jesus was telling them; in fact they were totally dazed by it all. They'd seen Jesus as a kind of hero, someone who could free Israel from the Roman yoke, and they'd even grasped that he was the Son of God, although I'm sure they didn't understand that bit too well either. Now something in their relationship was about to change dramatically. Jesus had always been someone outside of them, someone other, to whom they could look up in awe. But now this is all zooming up into a totally new dimension, the Son of God living in them—and they themselves living in the Son of God. And just to complicate matters further, Jesus is telling them about how they're going to get involved with the Holy Spirit.

I don't know about you, but I would certainly have struggled with that concept. It's taken me many years to come to such understanding as I have, and I have all Paul's writings to help me and I've listened to thousands of sermons.

What Jesus is saying through all this is that his followers are going to experience a new level of intimacy with the Father and him by means of the Holy Spirit. John obviously grabbed hold of this concept with both hands, even though his senses were reeling; here was a way to get even closer to Jesus—and his heavenly Father.

## Think about a vine

It comes as no surprise to us, knowing how Jesus operated when he was on earth, that he tried to clarify matters by means of a parable. "Just picture a grape vine lads ..." And so we find this parable sandwiched in between these two fantastic chapters.

> *"I am the vine, the Father is the gardener."*
> *"Remain in me, and I will remain in you."*
> *"I am the vine, you are the branches."*
> *"If you remain in me, and my words remain in you ..."*
> *"You are my friends ... no longer servants."*

J.B. Phillips translates John 15:5 like this:

> *"It is the man who shares my life*
> *and whose life I share who proves fruitful."*

We're talking intimacy here, folks. We're talking about the flowing of the life of Jesus into us, with all the implications that brings, as covered in the chapter *Intimacy and Ministry.*

## Paul's Grand Theme

Just in case you thought that John had a monopoly on all this teaching, we'd better now have a look at Paul. He often used an expression in his letters (all of them except 2 Thessalonians), in fact it was his favourite expression—*in Christ*. In some cases he uses this expression merely as another way of saying *Christian*, but usually he is using it to express a very intimate relationship, that of a shared life with the risen Jesus. In this context he never talks of our being 'in Jesus', indicating his emphasis of a relationship with a *risen* Lord.

Paul makes a definitive statement in Galatians 2:20.

> *I have been crucified with Christ*
> *and I no longer live,*
> *but Christ lives in me.*

This was the basis of Paul's life, and it sounds a bit like Jesus' statement in John 14:10, which we looked at earlier.

> *"Don't you believe that I am in the Father,*
> *and that the Father is in me?*
> *The words I say to you are not just my own.*
> *Rather, it is the Father, living in me, who is doing his work."*

Paul also states another very important principle in the verse above, namely that for us fully to share the life of Jesus we have to do some dying to our own life. For the life of the risen Christ to fully operate in and through me my own life in the flesh has to be crucified; the two lives cannot exist together. The extent to which my life has died is the extent to which I can share Jesus' life.

There's a verse Paul uses in 2 Corinthians 5:17,

> *Therefore, if anyone is in Christ, he is a new creation;*
> *the old has gone, the new has come!*

For Paul the old life had gone so that he could fully share Jesus' life. This verse is often used to say, "If anyone becomes a Christian," but I think Paul is saying something more than that. He's talking about the transforming power of a shared life.

That's the way Paul lived his whole life, that's why he was so effective in his ministry. It wasn't Paul doing the work, it was the risen Christ sharing Paul's life and expressing himself through him. Paul says the same thing in a different way, but with the same meaning. He says in Galatians 5:16,

*Live your whole life in the Spirit ...*

Whatever that means in practical terms it sure sounds mouth-watering! That's pretty well what Jesus kept saying in John chapter fourteen, "... I am in the Father, the Father is in me ... you are in me and I am in you ... the Spirit will be in your hearts ..."

## God's Secret Plan for the Nations

Finally, in this chapter, let me draw your attention to a verse that sums up the importance of this intimate relationship of shared life. This is how J. B. Phillips translates it:

*Col 1:27*
*They (the saints) are those to whom God has planned to give a vision of the wonder and splendour of his secret plan for the nations.*
*And the secret is simply this: Christ in you!*
*Yes, Christ in you bringing with him the hope of all the glorious things to come.*

# CHAPTER 6

# Intimacy and Prayer

## The Joy of Prayer

Given the importance of prayer and the fact that so many Christians struggle with it, or at any rate, never come to a place of really enjoying prayer, let's ask ourselves why. Let me make here what I consider to be a very important statement, namely that <u>we will never effectively take on the burden of prayer until we've learned the joy of prayer</u>. I believe that this is where we need to start, on the basis that God intends us to enjoy praying. And that enjoyment starts with intimacy.

I wonder if the way we instruct new converts actually tends to hinder their approach to prayer. For example, we tell them about the four essentials of Christian living; read your bible, pray, join a church, and witness to others. Now these are very important things to do, but is there maybe a touch of legalism suggested in the way we approach it? You must do this or that. But do we teach our new converts how to develop intimacy with the Lord? If we don't then prayer will develop into the drudgery of ploughing through shopping lists.

I think that, if we lose sight of this aspect of prayer, we're always going to struggle with the burden of prayer. God's greatest desire as far as we are concerned is that we have fellowship with him. Of course he wants to meet our needs in answer to prayer, but it's just the pleasure of communion with us which is most important to him. What parent would be pleased if their child only spoke to them when he or she wanted something? Cupboard love we call that! So how do you think God feels if the only time we ever talk to him it's to ask for something?

In any case, even when we are praying into situations it's important that we're not trying to twist God's arm to get him to do something, whether it's for us or someone else. The basis of prayer, especially intercessory prayer, is that God lays his burden for the situation and we share the burden with him. As I once heard Suzette Hattinghe say, "God gives us the burden, and we pray it back to him."

A phrase being used a lot these days is that God is saying to us, "Seek my face, not my hand," and that sums up what I'm saying succinctly.

Here are two quotations which are relevant and powerful:

*The wise lover regards not so much the gift of him who loves,*
*as the love of him who gives.*
*Thomas a Kempis.*

*Let him also rejoice and prefer to seek Thee,*
*even if he fails to find an answer,*
*rather to seek an answer and not find Thee.*
*St Augustine.*

Later on we'll look closer at how to develop intimacy, but for now let's look at how God intends prayer to work.

There are two pivotal verses which we all know in Romans chapter eight, verses twenty six and twenty seven.

*In the same way, the Spirit helps us in our weakness.*
*We do not know what we ought to pray for,*

> *but the Spirit himself intercedes for us*
> *with groans that words cannot express.*
> And he who searches our hearts knows the mind of the Spirit,
> because the Spirit intercedes for the saints in accordance with God's will.

There are four critical points in these verses., namely,

1. We don't know what to pray for.
2. The Holy Spirit knows God's heart.
3. The Spirit communicates that to us.
4. The Spirit actually does the groaning.

One translation puts it like this, '... the Holy Spirit Himself goes to meet our supplication ...' So it's not a case of my going to God with a list of demands, or suggestions about what he might like to do in certain situations. Nor is it a case of trying to twist the arm of a reluctant God. If we don't understand properly the parable of the persistent widow, or the man who wanted bread at midnight, we will think along those lines. No, it's a case of my knowing him so well, and being so attuned to his will—his heart and mind—that I'm praying what he wants. I'm actually partnering God in his desires.

A statement that Jesus made more than once has caused a lot of Christians to ask serious questions. It occurs in John 15:7 and it says:

> *"If you remain in me and my words remain in you,*
> *ask whatever you wish, and it will be given you."*

John says pretty much the same thing in 1 John 3:22,

> *we ... receive from him anything we ask ...*

Can that really be true, anything thing we ask for we can have? How many of us have tried that and found it doesn't work. So was Jesus just hyping it up? I don't think so. We're in fact back to the verse in Romans chapter eight, the one that talks about our not knowing what to pray for, but the Spirit does. So when we are sensitive to the Spirit we find ourselves praying what God wants us to pray for. These are the things that God wants to do, and it's nothing to do with our own natural wants. It seems a strange way to work, but that's the way God intends his work to progress. It's along the same lines I talked about earlier in connection with Adam and the work God gave him to do. God was involving Adam in his business, it was all part of the maturing into sonship.

So truly effective prayer is about bringing our wills into line with God's will and praying God's will into being. What was it Jesus said in the Lord's Prayer?

*"Your kingdom come,*
*your will be done on earth*
*as it is in heaven."*

True prayer is bringing about the reality of God's kingdom on earth.

When we groan in travailing prayer we're actually allowing God to express himself through us by means of the Holy Spirit. We're not only expressing his will (mind) but his emotions (heart), and how can we do this if we're not in intimate relationship with him?

So, to sum up this section, we can say that true prayer starts off in intimacy with the Father and with Jesus. It is true, deep communion between us, and from that communion come joy and the communication of God's heart and mind. And therein lies the secret of effective praying.

Here's a verse, part of which is well known, and the other half not so well known. That really is a pity because the first part of the verse is essential to the fulfilment of the second half. Isaiah 56:7 says:

> "... *these I will bring to my holy mountain*
> *and give them <u>joy in my house of prayer</u>.*
> *Their burnt offerings and sacrifices will be accepted on my altar;*
> *for my house will be called a <u>house of prayer</u> for all nations."*

When there is *joy* in the house of prayer, then people will stream to the house of prayer. The effectiveness and enjoyment in prayer have everything to do with intimacy. From a place of intimacy we become an expression of the Father's heart on earth.

## Esther—intimacy and requests

The story of Esther has some valuable lessons for us here. Let's start off in chapter five. You'll remember how Haman plotted against the Jews and managed to get King Xerxes to sanction a pogrom. Queen Esther's uncle, Mordecai, persuades her to approach the king to reverse the decision. Esther very clearly makes the point that she can't just walk into the king without prior invitation. That would be to risk her life. Nevertheless she does go in unbidden and the king holds out to her his sceptre as a mark of approval—and confirmation that she isn't about to die!

How did this come about? We have to go back a bit to find out but it isn't difficult because we see Esther is a most beautiful and charming woman. So Xerxes chooses her above all the other beautiful candidates for queen. However, these young ladies weren't just taken off the street and immediately presented to the king. Listen to what had to happen before they ever got near the king (Esther 2:12-14).

*Before a girl's turn came to go in to King Xerxes, she had to complete*
*twelve months of beauty treatments prescribed for the women, six*
*months with oil of myrrh and six with perfumes and cosmetics.*
*And this is how she would go to the king:*
*Anything she wanted was given to her*
*to take with her from the harem to the king's palace.*
*In the evening she would go there and in the morning return to another*
*part of the harem to the care of Shaashgaz,*
*the king's eunuch who was in charge of the concubines.*
*She would not return to the king unless he was pleased with her and*
*summoned her by name.*

Some fuss and bother that was, not a hurried throwing on a pretty dress, or even a quick shower; this was a full year's treatment before Esther even got sight of the king. Could that have something to do with how she was accepted by Xerxes—not forgetting God's grace, of course. The reception she got was terrific, as we see in chapter five, verse thee:

*Then the king asked,*
*"What is it, Queen Esther? What is your request?*
*Even up to half the kingdom, it will be given you."*

Esther didn't even need to break sweat (apart from nervousness as to what might happen to her), no desperate pleading or intercession. I think the reason is quite straightforward—the answer came because of the couple's level of intimacy. And that intimacy cost a full year of preparation.

Could it be that, so often, we sweat our way through sessions of intercession simple because we don't have the level of intimacy we need? I'm not saying that we shouldn't be interceding, especially since true intercession comes from an entering into the heart of God for a particular situation and sharing the burden of his heart. But I wonder...

Remember what we read in Exodus 33:11 a little while ago?

> *The LORD would speak to Moses face-to-face,*
> *as a man speaks with his friend.*

Could it be that so often we're banging on God's door for admission when, if we'd taken the time to develop intimacy we could have saved a lot of time and effort? John 15:13-16 links together the theme of friendship (intimacy) and answered prayer:

> *"Greater love has no-one than this, that he lay down*
> *his life for his friends.*
> *You are my friends if you do what I command.*
> *I no longer call you servants,*
> *because a servant does not know his master's business.*
> *Instead, I have called you friends, for everything that I learned from my*
> *Father I have made known to you.*
> *You did not choose me, but I chose you and appointed you to go and*
> *bear fruit—fruit that will last.*
> *Then the Father will give you whatever you ask in my name."*

Close friendship means that the two parties think alike and want to please each other. That, I believe is the key to effective prayer.

I'm also fascinated by Hegai's role in chapter two. He was the king's eunuch who was in charge of the harem. He would know very well what kind of young woman was likely to please the king (blonde/brunette, tall & slim/plump and cuddly, fun loving/ serious). He also knew what kinds of beauty treatments to use and when the young women were ready to go into the king. He would also probably have an idea of the king's mood at any one time. If we look at verse nine we can see that Hegai's role was vitally important as far as Esther was concerned.

*The girl pleased him and won his favour.*
*Immediately he provided her with her beauty treatments*
*and special food.*
*He assigned to her seven maids selected from the king's palace*
*and moved her and her maids into the best place in the harem.*

We could say that Hegai's role was similar to that of the Holy Spirit. He knows exactly what is on the Father's heart and how we should approach him. Truly effective prayer cannot happen without the Holy Spirit.

## Praying with a pure heart

Some time ago I was lying in bed shortly before getting up. As I lay there this very well known verse started running through my head.

But seek first his kingdom and his righteousness,
and all these things will be given to you as well.
Matthew 6:33

As I pondered the verse I began to see a new facet of prayer. Usually we think that praying with a pure heart is ensuring we have no known, unrepented sin in our lives because that will hinder our praying effectively. That is, of course, true but I think there's something else in praying with a pure heart.

I ask myself a simple question before praying for something or somebody, namely, what is my real motive for praying? Is it really for Christ's sake or because I'm unhappy with what's happening? Am I praying out of my frustrations or my own desires? Now I don't want to lose sight of God's promises to meet our needs, and I'm very aware of Hannah's pain as she prayed for a son (1 Samuel 1), but how much self interest is there in our praying?

It's so easy to sign off our prayers with, "For your glory, Lord," or "For Christ's sake, amen." But how real are we with these statements? It's important to realise that God is not reluctant to answer our prayers nor do we have to twist his arm—if we're praying from a place of intimacy with a pure heart.

## Priorities in the Pain

Of course, it's not easy to put the interests of Jesus before ours, especially when our hearts are in pain. For example, when we have loved ones who are not following Jesus and who may be messing up their lives. But, and it's essential to grasp this, his desires for wayward people are stronger than ours—even for our own families. You see, they're his before they're ours: he has a prior claim on them because he gave his life for them.

Are we prepared to subordinate our pain to his pain? He feels it more strongly than we do. I believe that truly effective praying occurs when we enter into Jesus' pain for lost mankind. When that happens we are sharing in his intercession as we experience the 'fellowship of his sufferings' (Philippians 3:10). That's what it means to pray, to ask, in his name.

So I see praying with a pure heart as being divested of every shred of self interest so that we are truly sharing in prayer with God's great redemptive plan for mankind. And this can only happen as we become progressively more intimate with Christ.

The reward is to stand with Christ as he intercedes with the Father.

*Psalm 24:3,4*
*Who may ascend the hill of the LORD?*
*Who may stand in his holy place?*
*He who has clean hands and a pure heart,*
*who does not lift up his soul to an idol or swear by what is false.*

## Two quotations to speed us on our way

How many of us pray without regard to the persons, but with regard to only one Person—Jesus Christ?
Oswald J. Chambers—*My Utmost for His Highest*

When I go to heaven's bank in the name of the Lord Jesus, with a cheque drawn upon the unsearchable riches of Christ, God demands that I shall be a worthy recipient. Not 'worthy' in the sense that I can merit or deserve anything from a holy God—but worthy in the sense that I am seeking the gift not for my own glory or self-interest, but only for the glory of God.

Otherwise I may pray and not get. "Ye ask and receive not, because ye ask amiss that ye may spend it in your pleasures" (James 1, verse 3, RV).

The great Heavenly Banker will not cash cheques for us if our motives are not right. Is not this why so many fail in prayer? Christ's name is the revelation of His character.

To pray 'in His name' is to pray in His character, as His representative sent by Him: it is to pray by His Spirit and according to His will; to have His approval in our asking, to seek what He seeks, to ask help to do what He Himself would wish to be done, and to desire to do it not for our own glorification, but for His glory alone. To pray 'in His name' we must have identity of interests and purpose. Self and its aims and desires must be entirely controlled by God's Holy Spirit, so that our wills are in complete harmony with Christ's will.

We must reach the attitude of St. Augustine when he, cried, "O Lord, grant that I may do Thy will as if it were my will, so that Thou mayest do my will as if it were Thy will."

*The Kneeling Christian*—anon.

# CHAPTER 7

# Intimacy and Ministry

Very often the two concepts of intimacy and ministry would be seen as poles apart. On the one hand we visualise the man who is in perpetual motion trying to get things done, and on the other, in complete contrast, the mystic, who seeks intimacy with God in a world of his own, detached from the real world. These two states of being are seen as being mutually exclusive.

We may call to mind the story of Martha and Mary, whom we often see as typifying the workaholic servant versus the dreamy worshipper. We may ask which one is right. Well, both, really, and an understanding of the relationship between the two is so important.

## Producing fruit

Jesus said in John 15:16 that we have been appointed to produce much fruit. But what is fruit? In Galatians five Paul talks about the fruit of the Spirit, which is clearly about character in that case. But there's also another explanation of fruit bearing, i.e. productivity. This can means soul-winning or producing worthwhile results in whatever work we do for God, as Paul explains in Colossians 1:10:

*And we pray this in order that you may live a life worthy of the Lord*
*and may please him in every way:*
*bearing fruit in every good work, growing in the knowledge of God,*

Earlier in the chapter (verse six) Paul puts it another way:

*All over the world this gospel is bearing fruit and growing,*
*just as it has been doing among you since the day you heard it*
*and understood God's grace in all its truth.*

Here's one more verse, just for good measure, Matthew 13:8:

*Still other seed fell on good soil, where it produced a crop—*
*a hundred, sixty or thirty times what was sown.*

Either way, there's one thing in common—neither form of fruit, character formation or productivity, can be produced by hard work and human endeavour. In the framework of the theme of this chapter what we're looking at is productivity, not character, so let's press on with this aspect.

John chapter fifteen is one of the pivotal passages for this theme, so let's look at a few verses from it.

*4 Remain in me, and I will remain in you.*
*No branch can bear fruit by itself; it must remain in the vine.*
*Neither can you bear fruit unless you remain in me.*
*5 "I am the vine; you are the branches.*
*If a man remains in me and I in him, he will bear much fruit;*
*apart from me you can do nothing.*
*7 If you remain in me and my words remain in you,*
*ask whatever you wish, and it will be given you.*

*8 This is to my Father's glory, that you bear much fruit,*
*showing yourselves to be my disciples.*

Earlier we looked at J.B. Phillips' rendering of one of the sentences in verse five, where he puts it:

*It is the man who shares my life*
*and whose life I share who proves fruitful.*

The secret of fruitfulness, of productivity, of successful service, according to this discourse of Jesus is not hard work, but 'abiding' in him. In other words fruit is a product of intimate relationship with Jesus. With a vine (or any other tree for that matter) if there's the minutest gap between a branch and the rest of the tree, the branch just dies, and certainly can't produce fruit. The branch does nothing at all to produce the fruit; it's the life of the vine flowing through the branches that does the job. The branches are there only to hang the fruit on, only as conduits for the sap, which is the transfer of the life of the vine.

In a man/woman relationship fruit (children) doesn't come from hard work—it comes from relationship, intimacy. That's a principle that God has built into humanity; it doesn't change in spiritual matters. Yet often we run around like crazy trying to make things happen whilst neglecting that which will produce the fruit—intimacy with Jesus.

And, of course, there's another problem; if we're not transmitting the life of Jesus, whose life are we passing on? Ours. How useful is that to other people? What eternal value is that kind of life? The words wood, hay and stubble spring readily to mind. So if we're running around like headless chickens, merely expending our own energy through our own efforts, then the odds are that we're not going to produce a lot of fruit. And much of that will probably not last too long.

I mentioned earlier the case of the prodigal son, and how his service for his father was on a different level when he returned, a service based on love and intimacy. How much more effective would that be than that of the hired servants? He would be reflecting his father's desires so closely that his service would be worth its weight in gold. Jesus expresses this theme a bit differently in John 15:14,15:

*You are my friends if you do what I command.*
*I no longer call you servants,*
*because a servant does not know his master's business.*
*Instead, I have called you friends,*
*for everything that I learned from my Father I have made*
*known to you.*

This time it's the intimacy of a close friendship, but the same end product: knowing the mind and heart of the friend and working from that basis.

This was how Jesus worked whilst on earth and it was the reason for his fruitfulness. Here are a couple of verses to demonstrate the basis of Jesus' ministry:

*Don't you believe that I am in the Father,*
*and that the Father is in me?*
*The words I say to you are not just my own.*
*Rather, it is the Father, living in me, who is doing his work.*
*John 14 :10*

*"I am telling you what I have seen in the Father's presence."*
*John 8:38*

*"I tell the things which I have seen & learned at my Father's side."*
*John 8:38 (Amp)*

In those two verses you have the distilled essence of the ministry of Jesus. The only way to see what the Father is doing and hear what he is saying is to get as close to him as possible. Otherwise we do our own thing and say our own words, and how useful are they? That last line of John 14:10 says it all. *It is the Father, living in me, who is doing his work.*

In chapter four we looked at 1 John 1:1-4 and John's excitement about the revelation of Jesus and his relationship with him a relationship which had developed since his first call to be a disciple. I wonder what would come across to someone who didn't know Christ as John shared his testimony with them? I'm sure he'd communicate more than just bare facts; there'd be communication at a deeper level than that.

How often do we merely tell stories when sharing the gospel with other people instead of imparting the intimacy which we have with Jesus. There's a big difference between the two. "Sharing Jesus" is more than merely talking about him. It's about passing on the life which we ourselves have in him. That's true ministry.

Let's go back to Jesus' ministry again, and about doing only what he saw his Father doing. We often think about Jesus healing all those who brought to him with physical and mental problems etc. Luke, however, tells us what Jesus often did on such occasions (Luke 5:16)

*But Jesus __often__ withdrew to lonely places and prayed.*

Jesus wasn't responding primarily to the needs of the people, but to the desires of his Father's heart. Makes you think, doesn't it? Not being close to the Father could involve our spending time and energy (fruitlessly maybe) in stuff we're not supposed to get involved with.

Some years ago I was in a prayer meeting with just a few other people. During that time one of the men described a picture which God gave him. In the picture were two men, one in a butcher's apron, the other in the robes of an Old Testament priest. The explanation of the picture was that both were ostensibly doing the same job—killing animals for their meat. But there was a significant difference; one, the butcher was cutting up meat to satisfy the demands of the people. The priest, however, was cutting up meat as an act of worship to God. The meaning was clearly given; when you work primarily to satisfy the demands of the people you will fail, but if you work primarily as an act of worship then God will meet the needs of the people through you.

## Authority

Where does true authority in ministry come from? It's that which takes us beyond just talking and doing to a dimension where people and situations are changed. Let's look at what happened in Acts chapter nineteen with Paul and the sons of Sceva. You'll remember that this was when Paul worked extraordinary miracles, casting out many demons. The seven sons of Sceva thought that this was great and all you had to do was to use the formula, 'in the name of Jesus', and out would come the demons. Here's how the great adventure turned out.

*Some Jews who went around driving out evil spirits tried to invoke the name of the Lord Jesus over those who were demon-possessed.*
*They would say, "In the name of Jesus, whom Paul preaches, I command you to come out."*
*Seven sons of Sceva, a Jewish chief priest, were doing this.*
*[One day] the evil spirit answered them, "Jesus I know, and I know about Paul, but who are you?"*

> *Then the man who had the evil spirit jumped on them and*
> *overpowered them all.*
> *He gave them such a beating that they ran out of the house*
> *naked and bleeding.*

This wasn't quite what these young men were expecting because it wasn't about a formula but a relationship.

*"Jesus I know, and I know about Paul, but who are you?"*

It's whom we know, and how well we know him that counts.

Let me take you back to Joy Dawson and *Intimate Friendship with God* again. In that same passage which I quoted earlier she goes on to say,

> Anyone with a natural ability to communicate can speak with liberty, but not necessarily have any spiritual authority. Authority from God is released only to those whose activity originates from God and is energised by Him. Then and then only can God receive the glory...
>
> Many times people confuse forceful speaking and eloquence, even when truth is being conveyed, with spiritual authority. Only what is spoken with God's authority will touch men's spirits and motivate them to take the necessary steps of obedience that will change their lives. All else touches only the intellect and/or the emotions....
>
> ... Only the right person at the right place at the right time, in the right condition of heart toward God and men, saying and doing the right

things, can believe God for the right results. It takes time to seek God to make sure these conditions are fulfilled. But the reward is a life of co-ordination and fulfilment.

To the degree we choose to live in submission, availability, dependence, obedience, and faith to the Lord Jesus, He will release His authority to us in the same way the Father did to the Son.

In his book *I Give You Authority,* Charles Kraft makes the following statements,

> One of the things God promises us is the right to use our authority to bring about whatever is in accord with His will (1 John 5:14). Our task is to get our wills lined up with the will of Jesus and the Father; and on that basis to exercise the authority they have given us.—This comes to us, as it did with Jesus, from spending time in prayer and fellowship with God in private, listening to him to get his instructions and to line up our wills with His. Then we receive from God the necessary power and authority for the specific task ahead of us. Our aim in our relationship with God should be nothing short of total intimacy. Again, Jesus is our model ...
>
> ... For me the biggest challenge in ministering to others is not in the area of power, but in the area of the intimacy of my relationship with the Father—a relationship that is essential to co-ordinate my will with His. Apart from an intimate relationship with God and an ear tuned to what He desires to do, our own authority-taking can

be powerless. What seems to put the power in our authority-taking, as it did with Jesus, is intimacy and hearing God. Together these enable believers to (like Jesus) do the works we see our Father doing. Discerning God's purposes packs our authority with God's power.

And Richard Foster has this to say in *Celebration of Discipline.*

When people begin to move into the spiritual realm they see that Jesus is teaching a concept of authority that runs completely counter to the thinking of the systems of this world. They come to perceive that authority does not reside in positions, or degrees, or titles, or tenure, or any outward symbol, The way of Christ is in another direction altogether: the way of spiritual authority. Spiritual authority is God-ordained and God-sustained. Human institutions may acknowledge this authority or they may not; it makes no difference.

The person with spiritual authority may have an outward position of authority or may not; again, it makes no difference. Spiritual authority is marked by both compassion and power. Those who walk in the Spirit can identify it immediately. They know without question that submission is due the word that has been given in spiritual authority.

Spiritual authority has nothing whatsoever to do with position, status, education or whatever; it's altogether to do with our intimacy with the Lord. Maybe that's what Paul recognised when he wrote these words in Galatians 2:6 (JBP).

> *As far as the leaders of the conference were concerned*
> *(1 neither know nor care what their exact position was:*
> *God is not impressed with a man's office) ...*

## Zeal without knowledge

How good it would be if only we could say that the church hasn't had a fair bit of egg on her face during her twenty centuries of existence, but, alas, this can't in all honesty be said. So much of the time she has lacked passion for her Lord and compromised with the world. At other times she has been very passionate—but has brought reproach on the Lord's name by her legalism, and in many cases, downright cruelty to those who didn't fit in with her expectations and rules. Let me take you back to some Scriptures we looked at earlier.

In John 8:54,55 Jesus says to the Pharisees,

> *"... my Father, whom you claim as your God ... you*
> *do not know him ..."*

So often we Christians have fallen into this trap. We claim the Father as God, yet, because we do not know his Father heart, we misinterpret and misrepresent him and much reproach has been brought on God because of this. We understand only part of his nature, and thus present an unbalanced picture, for example, holy but unfeeling or a sugar daddy. It's interesting that at the end of this discussion about Jesus' credentials the Pharisees wanted to stone Jesus, and he had to make a hasty exit.

Jesus covers the same ground again in John 16:2-4:

*They will put you out of the synagogue;*
*in fact, a time is coming when anyone who kills you will think he is*
*offering a service to God.*
*They will do such things because they have not known*
*the Father or me.*
*I have told you this, so that when the time comes you will remember*
*that I warned you.*
*I did not tell you this at first because I was with you.*

Oh, the dangers of knowing the facts, of knowing *about* God but not *knowing* him. There are things we would never do if we really knew the Father heart of God, if our hearts were beating in time with his. There can be many dangers in knowing the mind of God without having his heart. Paul made a simple yet profound statement at the end of his life. In 2 Tim 2:12 he said this:

*… I know whom I have believed …*

There's a world of difference between believing in Jesus and knowing him.

## Q.E.D.

Many years ago, when I was at school, I was taught geometry and we had to learn a number of Euclid's theorems. At the end of each one we wrote 'Q.E.D., which were the initials for the Latin phrase *quod erat demonstrandum*, meaning 'which was to be demonstrated' It signified that you had proved what you had set out to prove. So here's my Q.E.D. as regards intimacy and ministry, shown by some insights into the secret lives of some of God's servants who saw great fruitfulness. They were basically ordinary people, but people who had learned the secret of 'abiding' as Jesus described it in John chapter fifteen.

## Count Nicolaus Zinzendorf

Zinzendorf was the founder of the Moravian church in Eastern Germany in the early eighteenth century. In this community at Herrnhut was instituted a twenty four hour a day prayer meeting which continued for 110 years, and out of the community came the greatest 'modern' missionary outreach up to that time. It was through a group of Moravians that John and Charles Wesley found the Lord. Much of the Wesleys' early Christian experience was moulded by the Moravians and undoubtedly the Wesleys' early passion was role modelled by them.

Zinzendorf's motto was "I have but one passion; it is Jesus only." In 1727 the community at Herrnhut was visited by an outpouring of the Holy Spirit, and the presence of Jesus was so real that "They hardly knew if they had been on earth or in heaven", as one of them wrote. This intimacy with the Lord was the motivating force of all the Moravians' great exploits.

## George Müller

Few people are unaware of how George Müller provided for thousands of orphans in his orphanages in Bristol, in addition to other work such as Scripture and tract distribution. Appeals for money were never made either directly or indirectly. And yet the money kept coming in purely as a result of prayer and faith. In all he provided for over 10 000 orphans, distributed 2,000,000 bibles and 3.000,000 books and tracts, as well as giving aid to day schools both in the UK and abroad. He also gave over £260,000 to missionaries. The total sum of money received (and distributed—he had only £169 of his own money when he died) was £1,500,000, a huge sum of money in the 19th century.

What was the basis for this astonishing fruitfulness? In his excellent and insightful biography of Müller, Dr A.T. Pierson makes the following observations of his life and principles.

It was in the year 1837 that Mr Müller, then in his thirty second year, felt with increasingly deep conviction that to his own growth in grace, godliness, and power for service two things were quite indispensable first, more retirement for secret communion with God, even at the apparent expense of his public work ...

... conversion is not enough: there must be an *intimate knowledge of the Lord Jesus*. One must know the Lord as coming near to himself, and know the joy and strength found in hourly access. However it be done, and at any cost, the minister of Christ must reach this close relationship. It is an absolute necessity to peace and power.

*Growth in happiness and love* was next made very prominent. It is impossible to set limits to the experience of any believer who casts himself wholly on God, surrenders himself wholly to God, and cherishes deep love for his word and holy intimacy with himself. The first business of every morning should be to secure happiness in God.

He who is to nourish others must carefully *feed his own soul*. Daily reading and study of the Scriptures, with much prayer, especially in the early morning hours, was strenuously urged. Quietness before God should be habitually cultivated, calming the mind and freeing it from preoccupation. Continuous reading of the Word, in course, will throw light upon the general teaching of the Word, and reveal God's thoughts in their variety and connection, and go far to correct erroneous views.

## Smith Wigglesworth

Here was a man whose life straddled the nineteenth and twentieth centuries, and through whom God worked great signs and wonders. His faith, authority and power undoubtedly came out of his intimacy with the Lord, as these extracts from George Stormont's biography of Wigglesworth show.

> The Lord does not pour compassion into us the way we pour gasoline into our cars. It is released in our spirits as we are filled with the Holy Spirit and dwell continually in the presence of Jesus. That means being filled with God. Smith Wigglesworth's frequent prayer was to be emptied of self and filled with God ...

... Once he had heard a godly minister tell this story:

> There was a time in my life when I sensed that God was calling me to come apart and seek his face. But I was busy, and I would go on with those things that were keeping me busy. God was gracious and persisted in calling me. Bit by bit, I began to respond, until I formed the habit of going aside at the slightest breath of the Spirit to spend time with God.

This impressed Wigglesworth, and he developed the same habit. At home with his family or even in other people's homes, if he sensed a prompting in his spirit, he would quietly withdraw from company, go to his room, and enjoy the Lord's presence...

... Wigglesworth lived so close to God in the last years of his ministry He dwelt in the secret place of the Most High. Unbroken communion best describes his relationship with God. In that intimacy, he entered deeply into the experience of Jesus. He to saw what God did in heaven, then in Jesus' name he did it on earth.

# CHAPTER 8

# Intimacy and Revival

As we spend time in the Lord's presence, as we feel his heartbeat, we find that the sound that comes forth is "Revival." We don't pray for revival because we want it, but because God wants it! God wants his church to be normal. He wants it to be fruitful.

## Revival or What?

In a short paper I wrote with the above title some time ago I said this:

> I believe that one of the main purposes of God in sending revival is to cause the church to enter fully into a passionate relationship with her Lord, Jesus. Unfortunately, the phenomena become pre-eminent and in that I include the salvation of many souls. This statement may seem to some people to be heresy; however, I don't believe that God's main purpose with revival is the salvation of souls—that's the outcome of a revived church. In John chapter fifteen we're told that intimate living in Jesus produces much fruit—and that's what happens during revival. Somehow the

church doesn't seem to grasp that, the intimate relationship isn't maintained, and so 'revival' fades away.

I'm convinced that the reality of revival is meant by God to be maintained constantly. 2 Chronicles 7:14 says this:

> *"...if my people who are called by my name will humble themselves and pray and <u>seek my face</u> and turn from their wicked ways, then I will hear from heaven."*

I wonder if the problem is that we do seek God's face until he sends revival—then we've got 'it' and stop seeking his face. What he wants most of all is that we seek his face at all times, not just when we've sinned and need to repent. I believe that if we sought his face continually, and lived in the light of his countenance, then we'd live permanently in so-called revival. That doesn't preclude, of course, all the other ways that God deals with us, particularly as individuals, like, for example crucifixion and trials of our faith etc.

It's interesting to note that nowhere in Scripture are we told to "seek revival". However, God's people are told again and again to "seek my face". This, to me, is what it's primarily about. When we seek his face and find him then he fills our lives and we radiate his presence. *That* brings about all kinds of changes. If we get our eyes off Jesus then we miss everything.

Maybe we can learn something from the letters to the churches in Revelation. Of the two churches who got the sternest rebuke, one (Ephesus) had lost its first love and the other (Laodicea) was lukewarm. In neither case were they told to pray for revival, or any instruction remotely like that. In a word, they were told to repent and get restored to the place from where they had fallen.

When we come into an intimate relationship with the Father and Jesus we find ourselves having the same longings that they have. Often we groan, and this is because we are expressing the Father's heart, not primarily because revival is something that *we* want. The great revivalists have been groaners. We are longing for what God longs for, we are receiving God's heart through the Spirit.

The great revivalists have all had an intimate relationship with God. Revival hasn't happened because they were great preachers or teachers or leaders. It was because God had found a pipeline through which his power and blessing could flow.

Let's look briefly at three men who were instruments in revival.

## Count Nikolaus Ludwig von Zinzendorf

Count Zinzendorf, whom we looked at in the last chapter, was born in Dresden, Germany, in 1700 at a time when the Lutheran Church had largely ossified. However, a renewal movement known as Pietism had begun to bring new life, largely through Philip Spener, the 'Father of Pietism'. Zinzendorf came into contact with this movement when he was a student in Halle, principally through Hermann August Francke, one of Spener's pupils.

In 1719 Zinzendorf visited the art gallery in Düsseldorf and was arrested by a painting by Domenico Feti entitled '*Ecce Homo*', 'Behold the Man', being Pilate's words to the crowd as he led Jesus out to them. Underneath the painting was written the words, 'This I have done for you, what have you done for me?' Those words changed his life and henceforth his life was defined by this statement, "I have one passion; it is Jesus, Jesus only."

In 1724 a group of refugees, moved across to an area near Dresden which was part of Zinzendorf's estate. They had left their own country, part of what is now the Czech Republic, because of religious persecution, settling initially in a small village called Berthelsdorf. They became known as the Moravians after the area they had come from.

Not long after their arrival in Berthelsdorf squabbles broke out between them which threatened to destroy the community, at which point Zinzendorf offered them a new place which they named Herrnhut (The Lord's Watch) about three kilometres from the original settlement. The Count then set about trying to heal the rifts.

The following extract is an extract from John Greenfield's book, *Power from on High,* which is a history of the Moravians.

On 16 July 1727 the Count poured out his soul in a prayer accompanied with a flood of tears. This prayer produced an extraordinary effect. The whole community began praying as never before.

On 22 July many of the community covenanted together on their own accord to meet often to pour out their hearts in prayer and hymns.

On 5 August the Count spent the whole night in prayer with about twelve or fourteen others following a large meeting for prayer at midnight where great emotion prevailed.

On Sunday, 10 August, Pastor Rothe, while leading the service at Herrnhut, was overwhelmed by the power of the Lord about noon. He sank down into the dust before God. So did the whole congregation. They continued till midnight in prayer and singing, weeping and praying.

On Wednesday, 13 August, the Holy Spirit was poured out on them all. Their prayers were answered in ways far beyond anyone's expectations. Many of them decided to set aside certain times for continued earnest prayer.

No one present could tell exactly what happened on that Wednesday morning, 13 August 1727 at the specially called Communion service. They hardly knew if they had been on earth or in heaven.

'The Saviour permitted to come upon us a Spirit of whom we had hitherto not had any experience or knowledge. … Hitherto we had been the leaders and helpers. Now the Holy Spirit Himself took full control of everything and everybody'.

From that point the Moravian Church became one of the most pioneering and effective missionary movement the world has ever seen. A 24/7 prayer meeting was started which continued uninterrupted for 110 years. They stated, "No-one works unless someone prays," thus guaranteeing that, no matter where in the world their missionaries were, someone was praying for them all the time. Their watchword was, "Let us win for the Lamb the reward of his suffering."

Although Zinzendorf has been dead now for over 250 years his influence is still felt. John and Charles Wesley were influenced greatly by Moravian members of their ship's passengers by their calm in a fierce storm as they sailed to Savannah in what is now Georgia, USA. In fact the Wesleys visited the Pietists and Moravians in Germany after their return to England. It's said that Charles learned his hymn writing from them.

In the nineteenth century George Müller stayed for a while in the deceased Hermann Francke's orphanage in Halle and thus came under the influence of that same spirit.

## Charles Finney

Finney was born in 1792 in New York State. He was born again 1821, after struggling with conviction. Shortly after conversion, because he was having doubts about his conversion, he was seeking God. One lunchtime he had no appetite, but began to sing hymns, which was followed by weeping. Then, in the evening he decided to continue to seek God and the following two extracts describe something of what he experienced.

> There was no fire and no light in that room; nevertheless, it appeared perfectly lit to me. As I went in and shut the door after me it seemed as if I met the Lord Jesus Christ face-to-face. It did not occur to me then, nor did it for some time afterward, that it was wholly a mental state On the contrary, it seemed to me that I saw him as I would see any other man. He said nothing, but looked at me in such a manner as to break me down right at His feet. I have ever since regarded this as a most remarkable state of mind, for it seemed real to me that He stood before me, that I fell down at His feet and poured out my soul to Him. I wept aloud like a child and made such confessions as I could with my choked utterance. It seemed to me that I bathed His feet with my tears, but cannot recall that I had any distinct impression that I touched Him.

No words can express the wonderful love that was "poured out" (Rom. 5:5) in my heart. I wept aloud with joy and love, and I literally bellowed out the unutterable gushings of my heart. These waves came over me and over me, one after the other, until I cried out "I will die if these waves continue to pass over me!" I said, "Lord, I cannot bear any more!" Yet I had no fear of death.

Finney went on to be one of the greatest soul winners of all time. Over the next fifty four years he saw 1.25 million people saved—and 75% of them remained faithful all their lives.

## Frank Bartleman

On December 22, 1904, Frank Bartleman and his wife and two daughters moved to Los Angeles. He had a unexplainable impression that God was getting ready to do something wonderful in the Los Angeles area. For months he moved around the city visiting and preaching at various Holiness missions. During this time he also came into a deeper dimension of prayer and intercession. He had been corresponding with Evan Roberts, of Welsh Revival fame, and had received encouragement from him to pray for a mighty awakening in California. Soon Bartleman began increasingly to experience seasons of intense travailing prayer. One evening he and a friend, a man named Boehmer, decided to spend some time seeking God for revival and he describes what happened as follows.

After a little time of quiet waiting, a great calm settled down upon us. Then suddenly, the Lord Jesus revealed Himself to us. He seemed to stand directly between us, so close we could have reached out our hand and touched Him. But we did not dare to move. 1 could not even look. In fact, I seemed all spirit. His presence seemed more real, if possible, than if I could have seen and touched Him naturally. I forgot I had eyes or ears; my spirit recognised Him.

A heaven of divine love filled and thrilled my soul. Burning fire went through me. In fact, my whole being seemed to flow down before Him, like wax before the fire. I lost all consciousness of time or space, being conscious only of His wonderful presence. I worshipped at His feet. It seemed a veritable "Mount of transfiguration." I was lost in the pure Spirit.

For some time He remained with us … We had lost all consciousness of each other's presence while He remained with us. We were almost afraid to speak or breathe when we came back to our surroundings. The Lord had said nothing to us, but only overwhelmed our spirits by His presence. He had come to strengthen and assure us for His service.

All these were men whose greatest desire was an intimate relationship with the Lord; revival, in a sense, was a by-product of their intimacy. The first priority must always be, "Seek my *face*." When that is our priority all other things fall into place. Any other priority will distort the picture to a greater or lesser extent. As Eugene Peterson expresses it in his paraphrase of Colossians 1:16-18:

*Everything, absolutely everything ... got started in him*
*and finds its purpose in him.*
*He was there before any of it came into existence and <u>holds it</u>*
*<u>all together</u> right up to this moment.*
*And when it comes to the church, he organises and <u>holds it together</u>,*
*like a head does a body.*

Nothing works without Jesus, nothing fits into place or holds its proper place without him.

# CHAPTER 9

# Intimacy Through Scripture

There are many good reasons for reading the bible. Paul, writing to Timothy says they are "useful for teaching, rebuking, correcting and training in righteousness" ( 2 Timothy 3:16).

One of the principal ways of developing intimacy is hearing the voice of Jesus and of the Father. Praying is often regarded as talking to God for whatever reason; asking for things, complaining, etc. But listening without any agenda of our own is a quite different thing and is fundamental to growth in intimacy. Now, without doubt, God's principal means of communicating with us is through his word, as the Holy Spirit breathes life and revelation into it.

As we look into listening to God please bear in mind that in this chapter we are only looking at the aspect of developing a love relationship with Jesus and the Father. We're not talking about guidance, direction etc., although they're obviously very good reasons why we need to listen to God. There is nothing to compare with hearing the voice of the Lord. The experience of realising that he has communicated something of himself directly to us is one of the greatest thrills we can know.

For many years I'd been aware of the need to hear God's voice and made some progress along those lines. In 1987, however, God introduced a new dimension in listening to him into my life. In 1986 I'd had a poor year in business and wasn't earning enough to meet all the bills. At the end of that year, when business was quiet as usual, I set out to plan for the year ahead. I planned to work harder and smarter to boost my income. Then I seemed to hear God say to me, "No, you're not going to work harder. What I want you to do, in fact, is to work less. I want you to set aside one morning every week to spend quality time listening to me. What's more, this time isn't to come out of your leisure time but out of your working day."

God often has a habit of contradicting conventional human wisdom, and this was one of those occasions. I remember writing in my newly started journal (something else I felt constrained to start doing), "Can I risk this?" Then I sensed the Lord taking me to the story of Daniel and his diet. That's the time when he'd just been taken to Babylon and was to go on a very rich diet to be prepared to work for the king. He told the guard he couldn't possibly do that as it would displease God, and could he please stick to his very simple Hebrew diet. The guard was horrified, afraid that he would lose his life if Daniel (and his three companions) looked thinner than all the rest of the prisoners selected to work in the palace.

However, he agreed to a month's trial after which he would conduct a review of Daniel's appearance and fitness. At the end of that period, you'll remember, Daniel and his friends were fitter and healthier looking than any of the other prisoners. God told me that if I obeyed him he would honour that commitment. I'd like to say that I soon became immensely rich, but I didn't! However, the financial crisis passed and taking that half day out of business had no negative effect on my income. What it did do, though, was launch me onto an incredibly exciting journey of listening to him. It wasn't about intercession or making requests, but of simply learning to listen.

I've got to say that it very soon became a very enjoyable time, as I learned step by step the art of listening to the voice of Jesus.

And I'm still taking new steps, still learning, refining, making mistakes, taking risks, but I look back at the start of 1987 as a watershed in my life.

It's been very much about what is the most important aspect of our relationship with Jesus—relationship! That's what everything else revolves around—our relationship with Him. It's a love relationship, and that kind of relationship is about communication. One of the main things that God wants to communicate to us is His love for us. Now I know that the Bible tells us that God loves us, but He wants it to be more personal than just reading about it in a book. He wants to affirm His love for us—often. So the first, fundamental reason for listening to God is just for the sheer pleasure of doing so.

The question is, how do we listen? What are the practical steps in developing the art of listening to the voice of the Father and Jesus. I'm going to share with you some of the things that have helped me. Bear in mind, though, that it's not a formula; it's God you're listening to, not Keith Pointon. What sparked for me won't necessarily do the same for you. Be led by the Holy Spirit—we'll talk more about him later. Here, then, are some general principles.

1. <u>Ask God for the desire to listen to Him.</u>

The reason I say this is that we can't have any desires for God that He himself hasn't put there. We don't have time to talk about that just now; suffice to say that, if you haven't had any great desire to hear from God to date, you can't make yourself want to—but you can ask Him for the desire—then watch out!

That brings me to another crisis point in my life. In 1994 I had to undergo major surgery and I spent almost three weeks in hospital. During my recuperation period at home, which lasted several weeks, I became very concerned when I realised that I seemed to have lost my hunger for the Lord and reading my bible. Now this may have been due, in part at least, to postoperative stress but, nevertheless, I was very unhappy about it. It was just as bad, if not worse than, losing my natural appetite during times of illness. I discussed it with Christian friends but nothing seemed to help.

One morning as I was at home, by myself, I asked the Lord, "What's going on here? I can't bear to have lost my appetite for you and your word." Almost immediately an impression came strongly into my mind which I knew to be God's voice. He said, "I want you to realise that you cannot have any appetite for me except by my grace. Your appetite is a gift from me." It was a light, a bright light, shining and it started the process of the regaining of my appetite. It also opened a new understanding of the meaning of God's grace and caused me to make some theological adjustments.

2.  <u>Plan a time, place and how long you intend to set aside.</u>

There's one thing for certain, if you don't, you won't. In doing this, please, please don't start off by being overambitious; if you do you'll soon get discouraged. And it will all be different for different people. A busy mum with month-old triplets can't set aside the same time as a retired person, for example. Remember, this isn't some form of self-flagellation, it's actually meant to be an enjoyable experience, believe it or not. And I really mean that; I've found that these times of listening to God have been some of the most enjoyable times of my life.

3.  <u>Do remember that what you're setting out to do here is listen.</u>

It's not about coming to God with a shopping list, neither is it about heavy intercession (although these things are important).

If you have a close friend, or if you're in love, you don't have to make yourself listen to them—it's a pleasure. Primarily that's what this is about, listening to the 'lover of our souls. The first thing to do then is to …

4.  <u>Relax</u>!

One of the problems we have as citizens of the modern world is that we're always in a rush. Our minds are always in a whirl, and we need to do something about it. Here's an analogy you may find helpful. Let's say you've been out jogging and, naturally, you're all out of breath. What's the first thing you need to do? Get your breath back, of course! You really can't do anything else until you've done that. Now, in the same way, our minds are often out of breath; they're full of all kinds of things, so give them time to 'get their breath back.

One of the very important principles about listening to God is that it can't be rushed and peremptory. That doesn't mean necessarily that you have always to spend a long time doing the listening—primarily it means being ready and prepared. How? Here are some ways I found useful, particularly in the early days of this journey. Now I find it has become almost second nature to engage with Scripture and the Holy Spirit.

A principle I've followed assiduously from the beginning in this kind of bible reading is to use <u>only</u> my bible. I don't use commentaries or look at the notes in my bible. It's a time of going to the source of life himself without any other human input. However, if anything comes out of my reading that appears to change my previous understanding I will check it out later with other writers and trusted close friends. Checks and balances are important.

a. Spend a short time reading a book, preferably not a *heavy* Christian book.

b. Put on some background music.

c. Put on the answering machine, switch off your mobile phone—I'm serious! You need to avoid distractions. A book which I found very useful when I first started seriously listening to God was Joyce Huggett's *"Listening to God."* Let me quote to you a short passage from it here.

> Just sit down and relax. Slowly and deliberately let all tension flow away, and gently seek an awareness of the immediate and personal presence of God …You can relax and let go of everything, precisely because God is present. In His presence nothing really matters; all things are in His hands. Tension, anxiety, worry, frustration all melt away before Him, as snow before the sun. Seek peace and inner silence. Let your mind, heart, will and feelings become tranquil and serene. Let inner storms subside: obsessional thoughts, passionate desires, of will and emotions. Psalm 46:10 says, "Be still and know that I am God."

d. Have paper and pencil ready because you're going to begin thinking about all the things you need to do in the next few hours. If you write them down for attention later they're less likely to clog up your mind and distract you. Trust God to enable you to do them later.

e. A very practical problem about this approach is that you can be so relaxed that you can easily go to sleep! It's even better than counting sheep. If you do go to sleep, please don't castigate yourself, just say, "Sorry, Lord", and keep going. Don't lie on a bed of nails, but you may find that walking helps to keep you awake.

- Now ask the Holy Spirit to lead you in. As we saw earlier, he's the only one who gives us access to God's presence.
- Read a short portion of Scripture and read it slowly.
- Keep reading, repeatedly, until you sense God's presence, a sense of peace. Your mind need not necessarily be engaged at all at this stage; it's more like sensing someone is in the room, even if you can't see or hear them.
- If your mind wanders, don't feel guilty or panic. Just bring it to heel, and keep going.
- When you sense God's presence don't immediately rush on to something else. Just remain there. Keep silent.
- When you sense it's time to move on, do so. Maybe you could read a longer passage of Scripture. Maybe it would be right to worship or praise the Lord audibly.

It's important to keep at it, to keep 'practising the presence of the Lord', as Thomas à Kempis put it.

## 5. Keep a journal.

One of the most valuable tools I've found when listening to God is to keep a journal. It's not a "dear diary" kind of thing; I don't feel I have to write something in it every day. What I do is this; whenever something seems to strike me (and it doesn't even have to strike me hard!) I write it down. Very often it doesn't seem all that significant at the time, but it's surprising when I look back just how things tend to follow a pattern.

It's like joining up the dots in one of those children's puzzles. Having one dot doesn't make any sense at all; even having two, three or four doesn't either. At that stage it could be a dog, a house, or a jumbo jet. It's only when you've got a lot of dots joined that you can make out any semblance of a pattern at all. I've been amazed what a difference this simple tool has made to my life. So often, in fact, most of the time, God speaks in whispers, and we need to listen with care. A lot of what God says to us is missed because it doesn't seem significant at the time. And when it does seem significant we often forget or, at least, forget many of the details. If you haven't tried keeping a journal like this, try it; I'll guarantee you'll be amazed at how often God speaks to you, and how much direction there is in your life.

## Diligence needed

One thing for certain is that you will need to be diligent in your seeking intimacy with the Lord. One of the basic principles of natural life is that nothing worthwhile comes easily, and so it is in the spiritual life. Do you really think that God would give his best to those who can't be bothered? Is it reasonable to expect the one who gave his best, his only Son, to just drop the best of himself into our laps if it's too much trouble for us to seek him? I think Hebrews 11:6 puts it very well:

> *And without faith it is impossible to please God,*
> *because anyone who comes to him must believe that he exists*
> *and that he rewards those who <u>earnestly</u> seek him.*

Let's look at the parable of the pearl merchant that Jesus told in Matthew chapter thirteen, and allow our imaginations run around a bit. It seems quite reasonable to me to assume that, since this man was a pearl merchant, he had built up his own private collection of pearls over the years. I'm sure that whenever he got hold of an exceptional pearl he would keep it for himself; maybe just to admire its beauty from time to time, as an investment, for his pension or whatever.

But one day he comes across this pearl that stands out way above all his other pearls put together. In his heart grows this overwhelming desire that he must have the pearl, cost what it may. And cost him it would—everything, like the man in the previous parable who sold everything to buy a field containing buried treasure. So the man sells his existing pearl collection, possibly the finest and most valuable in the world, and he still doesn't have enough money to buy the pearl he desires. That means he has to remortgage his house and sell some stock (animals, that is, not company shares. Stock markets like that didn't exist in those days!) He finds that the only way he can raise the money is by selling *everything* he has. And sell everything he does, he's that desperate to get his hands on *that* pearl.

However, that isn't the end of it. Bear in mind he must have the cash in his hand to pay the man who is selling the pearl, which means that he has nothing but cash. Well, that's not bad, is it, you might reply. But wait. All his possessions, including his collection of pearls, are gone and he doesn't yet have his hands on *that* pearl. What if someone's beaten him to it? You see, if he has to go back and retrieve all his possessions and his pearl collection he's not going to get them back (if he *can* get them back) at the price he sold them at. He's going to have to pay a premium. Get the picture? This man is taking a colossal risk just to get hold of one pearl. And he's defying a fundamental piece of investment advice—don't put all your eggs in one basket. He's risked everything for the sake of one pearl. He's in no-man's land here. He's given up everything, and still doesn't have what he wants. What a colossal risk!

How much is knowing Jesus worth to you? Would you be willing to pay that kind of price to know him? As we saw earlier, this is how Paul put it,

*… whatever was to my profit I now consider loss for the sake of Christ.*
*What is more, I consider everything a loss compared to*
<u>*the surpassing greatness of knowing Christ Jesus my Lord,*</u>
*for whose sake I have lost all things. I consider them rubbish,*
<u>*that I may gain Christ.*</u>

## Keep focused

It's so easy to take our eyes off the goal. And one of the most common distractions isn't doing wrong, but doing right. Strange, isn't it, but the good can often become the enemy of the best. We can so easily get caught up in 'God's work', to the detriment of our relationship with Jesus. That's what happened to the church in Ephesus in Revelation 2. "You have lost your first love …" They were just too busy to love Jesus. Incidentally, if God hasn't told us to do something is it really God's work?

# CHAPTER 10

# Intimacy Through Obedience

Let's look now at developing intimacy from a different angle. So far we've looked at this aspect from a meditative angle, in other words sensing the Lord's presence by one means or another. This way of developing intimacy has a different feel to it, but I believe that it is fundamental, and in fact is the acid test of our degree of intimacy.

John is the man who develops this theme very thoroughly, which is hardly surprising since, as we've seen earlier, his intimate relationship with Jesus and the Father were the foundation and goal of his life. What may come as a bit of a surprise, considering how John liked to be close to Jesus, is how he defines the test of intimacy. Let's look at what John had to say, bearing in mind that love and intimacy are closely linked.

*If you love me, you will obey what I command.*
*John 14:15*

*We know that we have come to know him if we obey his commands.*
*1 John 2:3*

*But if anyone obeys his word, God's love is truly made complete in him.*
*This is how we know we are in him:*
*1 John 2:5*

*Those who obey his commands live in him, and he in them.*
*And this is how we know that he lives in us:*
*We know it by the Spirit he gave us.*
*1 John 3:24*

*This is love for God: to obey his commands.*
*And his commands are not burdensome,*
*1 John 5:3*

It's interesting that in these verses John makes no mention of sensing God's presence or the role of feelings. He says nothing about the "warm fuzzies" or the hair standing up on the back of our necks, or any other kind of feeling; in fact it's all rather sanguine—"The proof of your loving me is that you do as I tell you."

Of course, I'm not suggesting that the *sense* of God's presence isn't desirable—that would go against the whole flow of this book. Feelings, however, can be very fickle and misleading, so God has placed a cast-iron way of proving our degree of intimacy. It's a lot easier to say no to someone you hardly know than to someone you're very close to. It's a well known fact that a woman can get a man who is in love with her to do things no-one else in the world can!

These verses we've just looked at are talking about the proof and the result of intimacy; now let's turn it around and see what obedience produces. Let's go back to John again:

*"If anyone loves me, he will obey my teaching.*
*My Father will love him, and we will come to him*
*and make our home with him.*
*John 14:23*

Now I like the sound of that, that's what I'm looking for. What an incredible statement, to have the Father and the Son setting up home with me. Just look at the route to this place, though; through obedience. Despite what I've said earlier about how we develop intimacy, this is a totally different slant. The bottom line here is, *obedience produces intimacy with the Father and the Son.* This doesn't displace or supersede everything else I've written because all these things work hand in hand. After all, you can be disobedient if you're not hearing, and you can't hear if you're not living close, although God is known to shout from time to time!

In her book *I Dared to Call Him Father* Bilquis Sheikh talks a lot about the Lord's presence & his glory, and how to live in and keep his glory. Here's an extract.

> ... I learned to move back into his presence quickly. Whenever I did not feel his nearness, I knew that I had grieved him. I would move backwards until I spotted the time when I last knew his presence. Then I would review every act, every word or thought until I discovered when I had gone astray. At that point I would confess my sin and ask his forgiveness.
>
> *Through these exercises in obedience I learned the beautiful secret of obedience.* Repentance, I discovered, was not tearful repentance so much as admitting where I had gone wrong and avowing with his help never to make that mistake in the future. As I realised my own weakness, I could call upon his strength.

Notice the link between obedience and living in the Lord's presence; as long as Mrs. Sheikh was obedient she enjoyed the felt presence of Jesus. When she had been disobedient, as soon as she repented his presence was restored.

Jesus, of course, was the supreme example of this principle. We're all aware of his utter obedience to his Father, even to the extent of dying to the cross. Watchman Nee makes an important point when he says that Jesus' prime commitment was not to the cross, but to the will of his Father. It wasn't even his love for us (great though that may me) that took him to the cross; it was his love for, and therefore obedience to, his Father. As the well known verse says:

> *And being found in appearance as a man,*
> *he humbled himself and became obedient to death—*
> *even death on a cross!*
> *Philippians 2:8*

This principle had already shown itself in the life of Jesus earlier. We've all heard so many times that people thronged Jesus and he healed them all, but what about this verse?

> *… the news about him spread all the more,*
> *so that crowds of people came to hear him and to be healed*
> *of their sicknesses.*
> *But Jesus often withdrew to lonely places and prayed.*
> *Luke 5:15,16*

It's true that Jesus was full of compassion for people but that wasn't his main motivation; it was the desire to obey his Father and the intimacy that went with that obedience.

I think it's important to realise that this obedience is a *conscious* obedience. What do I mean by that? We have all experienced the leading of God in ways we haven't realised until we look back. In other words we have been *unconsciously* obeying God. There are, of course, times when this quite rightly happens. Some people think that that's the only way it happens, since they've never really learned to hear and discern the voice of the shepherd. I know good Christians who believe that God doesn't speak in discernible ways these days, which raises a very important question. How can we learn obedience if we don't hear from God what he wants us to obey?

We do have Scripture and that gives us a level, an essential one, of instruction to obey. However, there are all the various aspects of daily living where God challenges us to obedience, and it's in the response to these challenges that we have the opportunity to develop intimacy. Jesus didn't just use the Old Testament to decide when to be obedient, he spent many a long hour in communion with his Father finding out his specific will for that moment.

Jesus spelled it out again in John 15:9,10:

> *As the Father has loved me, so have I loved you.*
> *Now remain in my love.*
> *If you obey my commands, you will remain in my love,*
> *just as I have obeyed my Father's commands and remain in his love.*

In Matthew 7:21 Jesus made a very strong statement, and I'm not sure that I understand the full implications of what he said, but it emphasises the point of this chapter:

> *Not everyone who says to me, 'Lord, Lord,' will enter*
> *the kingdom of heaven,*
> *but only he who does the will of my Father who is in heaven.*

It doesn't come much clearer than that.

One of the things that really fascinates me is the relationship between people and dogs. I love to see a well-trained dog at his master's side, looking eagerly up to him, waiting for the next command. Then, at the command, how willing he is to obey. I've often wondered what goes on in their tiny minds when they're chasing and fetching sticks. Maybe they're just doing it to humour their owners! To watch a couple of hard working sheep dogs rounding up sheep is a particular pleasure. It's not that they just chase around; part of the task just involves lying low, panting, muscles taut, awaiting the next whistled or shouted command.

I've often wondered if that's how we should be responding to God. Then I've thought that it's maybe a bit insulting and demeaning to us. However, some time ago I was looking up the Greek word *proskuneo* in connection with worship; the word means literally 'to kiss towards'. Then I saw in Strong's that, in addition to 'to kiss the hand to (towards) one, in token of reverence' *proskuneo* is derived from a word which means 'to kiss, like a dog licking his master's hand'.

Now there's a thought! How does that sound to you? Am I taking things a bit too far, comparing us with dogs? I've got to say that I like the metaphor, and it reminds of the following verse.

> *I delight to do Your will, O my God.*
> *(Psalm 40:8 New King James Version)*

That's a picture of a Christian waiting diligently for the Lord's command as an act of worship—now that's beautiful. Maybe there's the same element also in this verse from Psalm 123

> *As the eyes of slaves look to the hand of their master,*
> *as the eyes of a maid look to the hand of her mistress,*
> *so our eyes look to the LORD our God,*
> *till he shows us his mercy.*
> *Psalm 123:2*

## A favourite prayer

One of my favourite prayers, and one I often pray, is one that Moses prayed as he made one of the most momentous choices of his life:

> *If you are pleased with me, teach me your ways*
> *so I may know you and continue to find favour with you.*
> *Remember that this nation is your people.*
> *Exodus 33:13*

Two aspects stand out very clearly to me in this verse:

1.  Moses is looking to develop further his intimate relationship with God through an increasing understanding of how he works. He's not content with having only pleasant, emotional experiences with God; he sees the development of the relationship coming through a greater understanding of the heart and thought processes of God.

It's like that with a married couple, especially after many years together. One of the signs of the intimacy of their relationship is demonstrated in an understanding of how the other partner thinks and the actions that please him or her. In fact, the thought processes of each spouse can often grow in similarity. Often with my wife and me one of us can say something to which the other will reply, "I was just thinking that." Scary!

It's one thing to observe what God does but it requires a deeper knowledge of that person to understand what's behind their actions. The following verse describes the difference between Moses and the rest of the nation.

> *He made known his ways to Moses,*
> *his deeds to the people of Israel.*
> Psalm 103:7

## Resonance

We all know stories about opera singers who can shatter a drinking glass simply by singing a loud note at the right pitch. The glass is pinged with the finger to produce its natural note and the singer then proceeds to sing the same note with the expected result. It's a matter of resonance—as the singer sings the glass vibrates so strongly that it shatters.

Some time ago, on television, I saw a bell maker demonstrate a traditional method of tuning bells. He took a tuning fork then struck it to produce the required note, after which he placed it lightly on the bell's surface. As he did do the bell began to resonate. The tuner explained that that only happens when the natural frequency of the bell matches exactly that of the tuning fork.

Can we say, as exemplified by these two illustrations, that we're so in tune with God's mind and heart that we resonate naturally with him so that obedience flows naturally from us. And it's important in this respect that we have not only God's mind but also his heart.

I believe there is a level of obedience which operates in the same way. At that level it's not just about obeying instructions but where we're in such a close relationship with God that we share his very heartbeat. We have not only his mind and thoughts but also share his feelings and passions. Whatever God thinks and feels resonates through our spirits and we find ourselves working in harmony with him.

Obviously the process of learning to live in this dimension doesn't happen overnight. It's a costly road involving the crucifixion of the flesh and our own desires, but what a dimension to live in. How much is possible to someone who lives at this level of intimacy and obedience? Surely this brings God's kingdom into every situation and enables his will to be done perfectly on earth as in heaven.

# CHAPTER 11

# The Cost of Intimacy

Nothing comes without a price; 'There's no such thing as a free lunch.' As we aspire to each level of intimacy there will be a price to pay, and at each stage we need to ask ourselves if we are prepared to pay that price. God, however, has a way of leading us in such a manner that we find ourselves coming to a place where God, having drawn us and shown us a glimpse of something good, then shows us the cost of going further. I think Jeremiah had that kind of experience, as he complains in Jeremiah 20:7

> O LORD, *you deceived me, and I was deceived; you overpowered me and prevailed.*

Strong's concordance gives some interesting alternative translations of the word *deceive*—persuade, flatter or allure. Have you ever been in that kind of situations with God, where you look at the price required to continue and you flinch? Have you found yourself unable to refuse because of what God has shown you in the way of enticements? I have!

Bob Mumford says it's as though God gives you a contract which is only a blank sheet. Then he asks you to sign it at the bottom of the paper, saying, "Just sign it and I'll add the details later." Only God could do that and get away with it!

I think there's a biblical principle here, which I call the *arrabon factor*. Let me explain. Ephesians 1:13–14 says this.

> *You were included in Christ when you heard the word of truth,*
> *the gospel of your salvation.*
> *Having believed, you were marked in him with a seal,*
> *the promised Holy Spirit,*
> *who is a <u>deposit</u> guaranteeing our inheritance*
> *until the redemption of those who are God's possession—*
> *to the praise of his glory.*

The Greek word, *arrabon,* here means 'money which in purchases is given as a pledge or down payment that the full amount will subsequently be paid.' (Strong's). Paul is actually quite fond of using this word, and it appears several times in his letters, always in the same context. It can also be used in the context of an engagement ring.

*Arrabon* is a foretaste, it's a sample of the whole, but only a sample. It's meant to whet the appetite, to lead us on. It's like the huge bunch of grapes brought back by the spies sent into Canaan (Numbers 13). It was an accurate indication of what was in the land, but it wasn't the land itself. It was a foretaste, an appetite whetter. After experiencing the sample we're intended to go in and possess the land, not just to enter, but to possess—to make it ours. We are not to be content with only a sample, a mere foretaste.

So it is with our developing intimacy with the Lord. He gives us further revelation of himself which thrills us, and then he asks us if we want more. When we say yes, then we begin to find out what the cost is, by which time it's too late to say no because we simply must have more of him! One reason for this approach from God is that, if we didn't receive a foretaste, we probably wouldn't be prepared to pay the price.

So what is this price then? Let's go to the verses from Philippians chapter three at the beginning of the book which are quoted in various translations (3:10–11, NIV).

> *I want to know Christ and the power of his resurrection*
> *and <u>the fellowship of sharing in his sufferings,</u>*
> *<u>becoming like him in his death,</u>*
> *and so, somehow, to attain to the resurrection from the dead.*

The first line sounds great—knowing him and the power of his resurrection, but the next line about sharing in his sufferings, and even his death, is a far different matter. This is where the rubber hits the road, so to speak. This is where we hit reality and are confronted with that hardest of all questions, "How much are you prepared to pay for increasing intimacy?" We've already seen (chapter three) what it cost Moses, David and Paul. For Moses it was a choice between intimacy and ministry, David found out what happens to intimacy when we sin, and for Paul it was:

> *I consider everything a loss compared to*
> *<u>the surpassing greatness of knowing Christ Jesus my Lord,</u>*
> *for whose sake I have lost all things. I consider them rubbish,*
> *<u>that I may gain Christ</u> ...*
> *Philippians 3:8*

## A question of holiness

One of the problems of this growth in intimacy is that the nearer we get to Jesus, the more we see ourselves as we really are. That means that we are increasingly confronted with our sinful nature—and that isn't pleasant. You see, we don't just see more sin in our lives, we also gain a greater understanding of just how repugnant that sin is to God.

Jesus expressed it this way in Matt 5:8:

*Blessed are the pure in heart, for they will see God.*

How can sin exist in the presence of God's holiness? 'In the year that King Uzziah died' (Isaiah 6) Isaiah certainly found out what it's like to get a close view of God. And David learned a sharp lesson after he had sinned in relation to Bathsheba and Uriah. Here's his well known prayer of repentance (Psalm 51:10-12).

*Create in me a pure heart, O God,*
*and renew a steadfast spirit within me.*
*Do not cast me from your presence or take your Holy Spirit from me.*
*Restore to me the joy of your salvation and grant me*
*a willing spirit, to sustain me.*

## A question of commitment

Then there's the question of commitment. Intimacy and commitment go hand-in-hand, or at least they do with God. That was always God's intention with physical intimacy between a man and a woman, hence marriage.

The spirit of the age is diametrically opposed to God's view of intimacy; nowadays what is demanded and expected is all the pleasure and thrills without commitment. And once we no longer enjoy these things with our partner we can always find another. Or we may even be totally promiscuous without any intention of even a short-term commitment. With Jesus and the Father this can never be the case, and each new level of intimacy will carry with it a corresponding demand from God for greater commitment and abandonment. As Mme Jeanne Guyon says in her book, *Method of Prayer:*

Abandonment is a matter of the greatest importance in our progress; it is the key to the inner court; so that he who knows truly how to abandon himself, will soon become perfect. We must therefore continue steadfast and immovable therein.

Or, as Basilea Schlink in her book, *Bridal Love*, puts it:

As a Bridegroom, Jesus has a claim to "first love"... Divided love is of so little value to Him that He will not enter into a bond of love with such a soul, for this bond presupposes a full mutual love. Because our love is so precious to Jesus, because He yearns for our love, He waits for our uncompromising commitment.

In *Christian Counsel* Francois Fenelon shows us where the pain really is:

God is a jealous God; if, in the recesses of your soul, you are attached to any creature, your heart is not worthy of Him: He must reject it as a spouse that divides her affections between her bridegroom and a stranger.

To abandon one's self is to count one's self as nought; and he who has perceived the difficulty of doing it, has already learned what that renunciation is, which so revolts our nature. Since you have felt the blow, it is evident that it has fallen upon the sore spot in your heart; let the all-powerful hand

of God work in you as he well knows how, to tear
you from yourself.

The origin of our trouble is, that we love ourselves
with a blind passion that amounts to idolatry. If
we love anything beyond, it is only for our own
sakes. We must be undeceived respecting all those
generous friendships, in which it appears as though
we so far forgot ourselves as to think only of the
interests of our friend. If the motive of our friendship
be not low and gross, it is nevertheless still selfish;
and the more delicate, the more concealed, and the
more proper in the eyes of the world it is, the more
dangerous does it become, and the more likely to
poison us by feeding our self-love.

We talked about obedience in the last chapter and obedience
is, in its essence, nothing else but the abandonment of my will to
God's. Obedience is a major part of the cost of intimacy; in fact,
according to some of the Scriptures quoted in that chapter it is
the ultimate proof of my love for, and therefore intimacy with,
both the Father and Jesus.

## A question of priorities

We're talking now not about the rightness or wrongness of
our actions, but their priorities. When we look at a list of the
*right* things we do, what is the order of their importance to us?
To increase the depth of our intimacy with Jesus, we can be sure
that seeking him must be the priority. It means ensuring that the
good doesn't become the enemy of the best.

If we're enjoying doing something, whether it's a leisure
activity or some kind of 'ministry' and Jesus says, "I want you

to come aside and just spend time with me," are we prepared to do that? I quoted the example of the young woman in Song of Solomon 2:5-8 in an earlier chapter. She was warm and comfortable in her bed and didn't want to get up again to let her lover in. How do we respond if the Lord wants us to get up in the middle of the night just because he wants fellowship with us? That's not convenient—but it's part of the price to be paid.

I've already quoted from Joy Dawson's book, *Intimate Friendship with God,* and here's another extract. She's talking here about the fear of God and what it can cost us, in the same way that it can cost us to seek intimacy with him.

> It can cost us many things to fear God and not men; being misunderstood, the loss of friendships, closed doors in ministry, rejection of many kinds, persecution, and even life itself.

There's no question that life can become lonely at times, as God calls us aside from the fellowship of other people. It has been said often that, the higher up a mountain you go, the less company there is. A mountain gets narrower as you reach its peak, and at times there's only room for you and God. But what is loneliness? Was Moses lonely on Mount Sinai? Was Elijah lonely in the cave, or was Jesus lonely when he spent time alone with his Father? There's loneliness and aloneness, and what's more important, fellowship with men or fellowship with God?

Yes, there is this kind of cost also; loneliness, misunderstanding and, sometimes, even a sense of feeling odd.

## A question of the cross

Unfortunately there's no easy way of dealing with the issues that are necessary to develop the intimacy of our relationship with the Lord. In fact, the cross is going to play the biggest part of all, because the flesh life, that which acts as a shield around us, has to be dealt with ruthlessly. Here are some of Paul's statements on this issue.

> <u>Put to death</u> ... *whatever belongs to your earthly nature ...*
> *Colossians 3:5*

> *I have been crucified with Christ and I no longer live,*
> *but Christ lives in me.*
> *The life I live in the body, I live by faith in the Son of God,*
> *who loved me and gave himself for me.*
> *Galatians 2:20*

> *But we have this treasure in jars of clay to show that*
> *this all-surpassing power is from God and not from us.*

> *We always carry around in our body the death of Jesus,*
> *so that the life of Jesus may also be revealed in our body.*

> *For we who are alive are always being given over*
> *to death for Jesus' sake,*
> *so that his life may be revealed in our mortal body.*
> *2 Corinthians 4:7,10,11 (Good News Bible)*

Time and time again we will be asked the same question as Peter, "Do you love me more than these." And often we will wrestle with this question and, hopefully, separate ourselves further in order to know Jesus more deeply. A.W. Tozer put it as bluntly as it can be:

> The old cross is a symbol of death. It stands for
> the abrupt, violent end of a human being. The

man in Roman times who took up his cross and started down the road had already said goodbye to his friends. He was not coming back. He was going out to have it ended. The cross made no compromise, modified nothing, spared nothing; it slew all of the man, completely and for good. It did not to keep on good terms with its victim. It struck cruel and hard, and when it had finished its work, the man was no more …

… If we are wise we will do what Jesus did: endure the cross and despise its shame for the joy that is set before us. To do this is to submit the whole pattern of our lives to be destroyed and built again in the power of an endless life. And we shall find that it is more than poetry, more than sweet hymnody and elevated feeling. The cross will cut into our lives where it hurts worst, sparing neither us nor our carefully cultivated reputations. It will defeat us and bring our selfish lives to an end. Only then can we rise in fulness of life to establish a pattern of living wholly new and free and full of good works.

This is not happy-clappy stuff, it's not about singing nice, gentle songs and experiencing the 'warm fuzzies', this is where it's at. Feelings can be so deceptive, both negatively and positively, and God knows that full well. Sure intimacy is about *enjoying* God's presence, but it's also about *enduring* the cross on the way there. Jesus, we're told,

> *... for the joy set before him endured the cross, scorning its shame,*
> *and sat down at the right hand of the throne of God.*
> *(Hebrews 12:2)*

To enjoy pure pleasure we must be pure. Is it worth it? Overwhelmingly, yes, as the Apostle Paul explains in Philippians chapter 3, which we'll look at in the next chapter.

# CHAPTER 12

# Gaining Christ

## Paul's 'one thing'

Many things could be said about the Apostle Paul, but one epithet that would fit him exactly would be *extremist*. In his early years he was an extremist for the Jewish law and customs; then came the incident on the road to Damascus. At the beginning of that day he started out as, in his words, 'a Hebrew of the Hebrews': by the end of the day he was well on his way to being just as zealous for Jesus Christ, whose followers he was hunting down mercilessly.

Why would someone change so dramatically? Why would Paul take up such a diametrically opposed cause so earnestly? The simple answer has to be that it wasn't a cause that was the issue: it was a PERSON—Jesus Christ.

Let's look, then, at Paul's relationship with, and dedication to, the person of Jesus Christ as he describes it in Philippians chapter three. Verse ten of that chapter is the basis, of course, for both the theme and title of this book.

It's important to note that, by the time Paul wrote Philippians, he'd been a Christian for almost thirty years, so he obviously wasn't talking about his initial new birth. Rather, it's an expression of the prime driving force of his life—an increasing knowledge of the person of Jesus Christ. The following translation from the

Amplified New Testament sums up the intensity of Paul's longing for more of Jesus:

> *… that I may progressively become more deeply*
> *and intimately acquainted with him,*
> *perceiving and understanding the wonders of his person*
> *more strongly and more clearly.*

Although Paul wrote much about theological and doctrinal truths, that statement was really what he was all about—a progressive, intimate knowledge of the person who had revealed himself to him. It's something that flows out of him continually, as we'll see.

## A seismic upheaval for Paul

Let's look first of all at just how radical that change was, that complete redirecting of his life. In the first part of Philippians chapter three Paul declares just how big a radical he is; let's look at his statements. But before we look at these statements individually we need first to look at the crowning verse of his declaration. If you ever wanted a clear, all consuming mission statement, then verse eight gives the consummate aim for every passionate disciple of Jesus. It's both the bedrock and pinnacle of what the Christian life is all about.

> *Phil 3:8.*
> *What is more, I consider everything a loss*
> *compared to the surpassing greatness of knowing Christ Jesus my Lord,*
> *for whose sake I have lost all things.*
> *I consider them rubbish, <u>that I may gain Christ</u> …*

We'll come back later to have a more detailed look at what Paul is saying in that verse, but first let's look at where he's come from, as he explains in verses five and six.

## Extreme 1

*Circumcised on the eighth day.* With this statement Paul is saying, "Not only am I a direct descendant of Abraham, but I am descended from Isaac, the son of promise." Ishmael was circumcised in his thirteenth year, whereas Isaac was circumcised when he was eight days old.

## Extreme 2

*Of the people of Israel.* Paul is again stressing his racial purity, for the Ishmaelites could trace their ancestry back to Abraham (through Hagar) and the Edomites could go back to Isaac via Esau. But the true Israelites were the ones who could go back to Jacob, who was renamed Israel after he'd wrestled with God.

## Extreme 3

*Of the tribe of Benjamin.* The tribe of Benjamin was regarded as being among the élite of the Israelite nation. For example, Benjamin was the only son of Jacob (Israel) who was born in the Promised Land. King Saul was a Benjamite. When the Israelites returned from exile the tribes of Judah and Benjamin formed the nucleus of the reborn nation. And a familiar battle cry of the nation was, "Lead on, O Benjamin." Hosea 5:8 commands:

> *"Sound the trumpet in Gibeah, the horn in Ramah.*
> *Raise the battle cry in Beth Aven; lead on, O Benjamin."*

### Extreme 4

*A Hebrew of Hebrews.* In saying this, Paul was affirming that he was more than just a pure bred Israelite. During Paul's time his fellow countrymen were scattered throughout the known world. As they settled into new countries they remained in tightly knit communities and diligently maintained their faith. However, it was necessary for them to learn the language of their adopted country in order to live and work effectively. In so doing the majority of them eventually forgot their own language, Hebrew. Paul was one who hadn't done that, maintaining his ability to speak Hebrew as well as Greek and Aramaic.

### Extreme 5

*As regards the law, a Pharisee.* Gradually Paul is moving to the sharp and narrow end of the élite strata of the Jews. By degrees he's been filtering out the 'lesser mortals' amongst his countrymen. We all know how strict the Pharisees were about the law, even though Jesus often called them hypocrites and used even stronger epithets on many occasions. There were never more than six thousand of them at any one time, so Paul is nearing the top of the tree in Jewish society.

### Extreme 6

*As for zeal, persecuting the church.* No one could doubt Paul's zeal for the purity of the Jewish religion, especially as they saw him hounding the followers of Jesus to prison or even death. He was driven by blind hatred of the people whose leader had come 'full of grace and truth', so demolishing the whole foundation of salvation by observance of the law as opposed to salvation by grace through faith.

<u>Extreme 7</u>

*As for legalistic righteousness, faultless.* What a claim!
Paul's defence to the Sanhedrin is recounted in Acts 22.

Acts 22:3,4
*"I am a Jew, born in Tarsus of Cilicia, but brought up in this city.
Under Gamaliel I was thoroughly trained in the law of our fathers
and was just as zealous for God as any of you are today.
I persecuted the followers of this Way to their death,
arresting both men and women and throwing them into prison,*

We have now a clear picture of Paul as an ultra right wing,
fully paid-up member of the Jewish élite before he did his
about turn.

## Turning profit into loss

For Paul, up to the point of his conversion, life was as good
as it could be considering his land was occupied by enemy forces.
Now, in verse seven, he makes this dramatic statement.

*But whatever was to my profit I now consider loss for the sake of Christ.*

Then in the next verse he tells us that he now considers
*everything* as loss compared to the knowledge of Jesus. Notice he
doesn't say anything about the *cause* of Jesus, he's only talking
about the knowledge of a person.

Now we need to look at verse eight again, this time in more
detail, to get the enormity of what Paul did those twenty nine
years earlier. The numbers given to the five headings following
the verse correspond to the superscript numbers I've inserted
into it.

*Phil 3:8.*

*What is more, I consider[2] everything a loss[3]*
*compared to the surpassing greatness[5] of knowing Christ Jesus my Lord,*
*for whose sake I have lost all things[3].*
*I consider them rubbish[4], that I may gain[1] Christ …*

1.  <u>That I may gain Christ.</u>

Let's focus first of all on the purpose, the goal of all this, and it's found in the last phrase of this verse: "… that I may gain Christ." Everything else hangs on this one statement, which is the determining factor in everything Paul does.

This word for gain (or win) is used in many different contexts in the New Testament. For example, Jesus uses it in the parable of talents, where it means to make a profit, to accumulate more. We find it also in Matthew 16:26, where Jesus says, "What good is it for a man to gain the whole world …"

Paul also uses the word when he talks about gaining or winning various groups for Christ—Jews, Gentiles, the weak.

Now this begs one or two questions. Given that Paul had been a disciple for almost thirty years and that this is a present action, he can't be referring to his conversion. No, Paul had made the original commitment, but the process just kept getting deeper. Paul is saying that he wants to know Christ in all his fulness. He longs to gain a very close, intimate relationship with Jesus. He often uses the expression, "Christ in you," or talks about our being in Christ. How important Paul's relationship is to Christ we'll see very shortly.

2.  <u>I consider everything (a loss).</u>

The word Paul uses here is the word of accountancy, where it emphasises that one should not make hasty decisions. It's a weighing up of all the facts then coming to a reasoned conclusion, just as an accountant would do when looking at a firm's accounts. It's also the sort of thing a mathematician would do. Having done that, he then decides that all these extreme advantages we looked at earlier were worth absolutely nothing and he was willing to write them off as a dead loss.

Although Paul had had such a powerful experience on the road to Damascus his decision to <u>gain</u> Christ was not made on the spur of the moment, nor was it based on his emotions at that time. He's considered carefully the nature of Jesus and then made his decision, and having done that there was no going back. No-one can be pressured into making such a decision.

3.   <u>The cost.</u>

When Paul uses the term 'all things' that's what he really means; it's not an exaggeration nor is he using it merely for effect. He really is saying that everything else in the world pales into insignificance in the light of knowing Christ.

4.   <u>The contrast.</u>

Now Paul uses a very strong descriptive word to express how little his former advantages in life were worth. The NIV uses the word 'rubbish', but that's too mild a word; it's for the squeamish. In other translations it's rendered variously dung, garbage, loss, refuse, dog dung (*The Message*), and sheer loss. Let's look more closely at the Greek word *skubalon* being translated here to get a more complete picture.

- Excrement—human or animal. The King James Version and Kenneth Wuest use the word 'dung'.
- Only what's fit to be thrown to the dogs.

- Offscourings.
- Street filth. That means all the rubbish that has been discarded in a busy street. Maybe, in days gone by (in Britain), it would include the contents of chamber pots discarded (to the cry of, "Gardy-loo") in the street.
- A half-eaten corpse. After a flood corpses of human beings and animals, half eaten by fish, would be washed up, stinking and repulsive, on the shore or river banks: that was *skubalon*.

This is Kenneth Wuest's comment on Paul's loss.

Paul was a citizen of Tarsus. At the time he lived there, only families of wealth and reputation were allowed to retain their Tarsian citizenship. This throws a flood of light upon Paul's early life. He was born into a home of wealth and culture. His family were wealthy Jews living in one of the most progressive of oriental cities. All this Paul left to become a poor itinerant missionary. But not only did he forfeit all this when he was saved, but his parents would have nothing to do with a son who had in their estimation dishonoured them by becoming one of those hated, despised Christians. They had reared him in the lap of luxury, had sent him to the Jewish school of theology in Jerusalem to sit at the feet of the great Gamaliel, and had given him an excellent training in Greek culture at the University of Tarsus, a Greek school of learning. But they had now cast him off. He was still forfeiting all that he had held dear, what for? He tells us, "that I may win Christ." (Wuest's

Word Studies from the Greek New Testament:
Eerdmans or Logos)"

Then having described how worthless all his former prized possessions had become to him, Paul now describes what has displaced them in value—*"the surpassing greatness of knowing Christ Jesus."*

The Greek word translated here by 'surpassing' is *huperecho* from *hupér,* meaning above or over, plus *écho,* meaning to have. The word means literally to hold above and so to stand out or be superior in rank, authority or power. *Huperecho* speaks of that which excels, is superior or better and which is exceptional or excellent.

Knowing Christ is of incomparable worth—of more value than anything!

Was it to gain eternal life and salvation from hell that Paul paid this immense price? No! It was to gain Christ. To be certain, the other things came with the package, but for Paul it was this increasing intimate knowledge of Jesus Christ that impelled him.

Paul's mission in life was to preach the gospel to the Gentiles, to go wherever the gospel had not yet been preached, but look what he wrote in Ephesians 3:8 about his call to preach:

*Although I am less than the least of all God's people,*
*this grace was given me:*
<u>*to preach to the Gentiles the unsearchable riches of Christ,*</u>

This was far more than just preaching a gospel of mere salvation: Paul wanted everyone to see Christ as he saw him and commit to gaining him. This comes out so clearly in some of his prayers for the churches he'd been involved in. Take time to meditate on what he's praying in Ephesians 1:15-19, 3:14-19 and Colossians 2:1-3. He wanted all Christians to be utterly consumed with the desire for an ever deepening knowledge of Christ. We'll come back to some of these verses later.

## How much are <u>we</u> willing to pay?

How much do we really want this experience of Christ? How deep is the longing in our hearts to gain him? The problem is, of course, that it comes down to cost, as usual. In Matthew 13:44-46 Jesus told two parables, both with the same thrust. First of all he said the kingdom of heaven is like a man who found hidden treasure in a field. Imagine how he felt when he found it. Jesus said he immediately rushed home and sold everything he had so that he buy not only the treasure, but the whole field. You can be sure he wouldn't have told anyone about it until he had paid the money for the field.

Then he talked about the merchant who found the immensely valuable pearl. He was so overcome with its beauty that he also rushed home, sold everything he had and bought it.

There is more than one common factor in these parables, but I'd like to highlight just one at this point, and that is the element of risk in what these two men did. You see, there was a period during these transactions when these men had nothing that they had valued previously, or were in the process of obtaining. All they had was cash. What if someone found the treasure before the field changed hands? What if someone else managed to get their hands on the pearl first?.

Jesus stated clearly and simply what it cost these men to gain what they really desired—<u>they sold everything they had</u>! That's how much the treasure and the pearl meant to them. How much is the knowledge of Jesus worth to you? How much are you willing to sacrifice to gain him? You're a good, committed Christian and a good person in general, but how far along the road of gaining Christ are you? How much are you prepared to pay for that knowledge? Are you consumed with the same ambition Paul talks about in Philippians 3:10, as expanded by the Amplified Version?

There is a cost, and the more we want to know and gain Christ, the more it will cost us.

> Salvation is free, it's all of grace.
> To gain Christ will cost us everything.

It is, of course, a progression, which Paul makes clear. In fact in Philippians 3:12 he emphasises that gaining Christ is for him still a work in progress:

> *Not that I have already obtained all this,*
> *or have already been made perfect,*
> *but I press on to take hold of that for which*
> *Christ Jesus took hold of me.*

It's obvious from the way that Paul writes here that the fulness of gaining Christ is not given to the casual believer. There is a price, a progressive price, that needs to be paid.

## Is it worth it?

5. <u>The goal.</u>

So what was it that led Paul to pay such a high price? What is so special about Jesus? Let's look again at Philippians 3:8. There Paul talks about the 'surpassing greatness of knowing Christ Jesus my Lord'. When talking about Jesus Paul is apt to use extreme language; after all he's gone from being an extreme zealot of Judaism to the very opposite extreme. He's gone from being persecutor to persecuted.

The Amplified New Testament translates surpassing greatness as,

> ... *the priceless privilege—the overwhelming preciousness,*
> *the surpassing worth and supreme advantage ...*

In Ephesians 3:8 Paul writes,

> *Although I am less than the least of all God's people,*
> *this grace was given me:*
> *to preach to the Gentiles the <u>unsearchable riches of Christ</u>,*

which the Amplified Version renders as,

> ... *the unending (boundless, fathomless, incalculable and exhaustless)*
> *riches of Christ—*
> *wealth which no human being could have searched out.*

In the phrase 'the unsearchable riches of Christ' Paul contains two facets of meaning, both of which are valid within the context:

1. The riches cannot be found by human endeavour and reasoning. The only way to find the treasure is as the Holy Spirit reveals it to us.
2. No matter how much of the treasure we discover, there is infinitely more yet to be found. The treasure is inexhaustible.

The fact that God has made it impossible to find these riches doesn't mean that he doesn't want us to; quite the opposite. But he will only reveal the riches to those who are serious and diligent. This is what Jesus said in Luke 10:21.

*At that time Jesus, full of joy through the Holy Spirit, said,*
*"I praise you, Father, Lord of heaven and earth,*
*because you have hidden these things from the wise and learned,*
*and revealed them to little children.*
*Yes, Father, for this was your good pleasure.*

In Greek hidden is *apokrupto*, being *apo* (away) plus *krupto* (compare crypt, the hidden part of the church; encrypt; cryptic). *Apokrupto* has the sense of being hidden away. If you like, God has encrypted his most precious treasures so that only those with the key can unlock them. That key is the Holy Spirit coupled with a diligently seeking heart.

Revealed is *apokaluptos*, which has the sense of taking off the lid. It's been adopted into English in the word apocalypse. God is very keen that each one of us strongly desires the lid to be taken off in order to reveal Jesus to us through the Holy Spirit. Then, and only then, can we in turn adequately declare him to the outside world.

## The reward

Paul explains to us what, or more correctly who, the reward is:

*Col 2:3*
*(Christ) … in whom are hidden all the treasures*
*of wisdom and knowledge.*

The really exciting aspect of these boundless, fathomless, incalculable and exhaustless riches is that they are just that! Nothing else in life has that appeal. We love music, but we need a constant supply of new tunes as we get bored with the old ones. Once we loved them, but now they no longer appeal to us.

It's the same with friendships so often, and with marriages and similar man/woman relationships. They're great when they're fresh and new, but can be discarded when the initial excitement wears off.

Children in the developed nations now have so many playthings that they don't really value them and they soon get discarded and stuck in boxes and cupboards.

But with Jesus, for those who are prepared to pay the price, there's a never ending source of discovery. No matter how much we discover by Holy Spirit revelation there's much more to come. Church meetings, service, causes, etcetera are not the focus here—it's *Jesus*.

The all-consuming passion of Paul for Christ had not dimmed after almost thirty years, rather it had grown. It was that same passion that drove him in his service for Christ, which was his worship. That's why he wrote Romans 12:1.

> *Therefore, I urge you, brothers, in view of God's mercy,*
> *to offer your bodies as living sacrifices,*
> *holy and pleasing to God—this is your spiritual act of worship.*

The Amplified Bible renders the last phrase as,

> *… your reasonable (rational, intelligent) service and spiritual worship.*

Again w can see that Paul isn't calling for a purely emotional decision: it's a decision made on the basis of the first eight chapters of his letter. And please note that this is worship. I regard this statement as describing the real heart of worship—sacrifice based on loving obedience. I wonder if sometimes (even often) we worship God because it makes us feel good. I believe there's always that danger if we regard worship as primarily singing songs.

In concluding this chapter I'd like to quote a couplet from one of my favourite songs:

> All consuming, all embracing
> Fervent God of love, enthral me.
> Chris Bowater

# CHAPTER 13

# In Conclusion

## A challenge

I've written this book, not primarily as a bible study, but as an account of my journey towards knowing Christ. It's been a challenging journey and sometimes a costly one, but it's a goal for me that has never dimmed and, in fact, it's now stronger than it ever was. And since that verse, Philippians 3:10, first hit me so long ago I realise at this point that I'm now almost fifty years closer to the reality of this next verse:

*At present we are men looking at puzzling reflections in a mirror.*
*The time will come when we shall see reality whole and face-to-face!*
*At present all I know is a little fraction of the truth,*
*but the time will come when I shall know it as fully*
*as God has known me!*
*1 Corinthians 13:12*

Then, I'm sure, I'll say with Augustine, "All I have written is but straw!" This is how John the apostle put it:

*Here and now, my dear friends, we are God's children.*
*We don't know what we shall become in the future.*

*We only know that when he appears we shall be like him,*
*for we shall see him as he is!*
*1 John 3:2*

What do you think? How will you choose? Let me finish with a verse of an old hymn. The words are maybe somewhat old fashioned but what's expressed in this hymn by F. Brook is so appropriate, not only for this chapter, but for the whole book.

My goal is God Himself, not joy, nor peace,
Nor even blessing, but Himself, my God:
'Tis His to lead me there, not mine, but His.
"At any cost, dear Lord, by any road!"

# Bibliography

I gratefully acknowledge the authors of the following works; they have contributed to the richness of my life.

Frank Bartleman, *Another Wave of Revival*, Whitaker House, Springdale, PA 15144, USA

Joy Dawson, *Intimate Friendship with God*, Kingsway Publications, Lottbridge Drove, Eastbourne BN23 6NT, UK.

Gene Edwards/Mme. Guyon, *Experiencing the Depths of Jesus Christ*, Seed Sowers Christian Books Publishing House, Auburn, ME 04212-3368, USA.

Richard Foster, *Celebration of Discipline*, Hodder and Stoughton, 33-34 Alfred Place, London, WC1E 7DP, UK

Joyce Huggett, *Listening to God,* Hodder and Stoughton Hodder and Stoughton, 33-34 Alfred Place, London WC1E 7DP, UK.

J.B. Phillips, *New Testament in Modern English*, Macmillan London Ltd, Cavaye Place, London, SW10 9PG, UK

Charles Kraft, *I Give You Authority*, Monarch Books, Broadway House, The Broadway, Crowborough, TN6 1HQ, UK.

Basilea Schlink, *Bride of Jesus Christ*, Evangelical Sisterhood of Mary, P.O.B. 13 01 29, D-64241, Darmstadt, Germany.

Bilquis Sheikh, *I Dared to Call Him Father*, Kingsway Publications Ltd, Lottbridge Drove, Eastbourne, BN23 6NT, UK.

George Stormont, *Smith Wigglesworth: The Man Who Walked with God,* Sovereign World Ltd., PO Box 777, Tonbridge, TN11 0ZS, UK.

Sammy Tippit, *No Matter What the Cost,* Word Books, 9 Holdom Avenue, Bletchley, MK1 1QR, UK.

Tommy Tenney, *The God Chasers,* Destiny Image Publishers, Inverse, P.O. Box 310, Shippensburg, PA 17257-0310.

Oswald J. Chambers, *My Utmost for His Highest,* Discovery House Publishers, PO Box 1, Carnforth, Lancashire LA5 9ES, United Kingdom.

Dr. A.T. Pierson, George Müller of Bristol, Pickering & Inglis Ltd., 26 Bothwell St, Glasgow, G2 6PA, UK.

*Fenelon's Spiritual Letters,* Christian Books Publishing House, Gardiner, Maine, 04345. USA.

John G. Greenfield, *Power from on High,* published in 1927 on the 200th anniversary of the Moravian revival.

Kenneth Wuest, New Testament Commentary.

F Brook, *My goal is God himself,* copyright owner Miss B Brook.

Chris Bowater, *All consuming, all embracing,* © Sovereign Lifestyle Music, P.O. Box 356, Leighton Buzzard, Bedfordshire LU7 8WP, U.K.

# Acknowledgements

I would like to pay tribute to some people whose contributions to my life have been very significant. Many people have had important input, which I greatly appreciate, but these few people's input have helped shape me.

My mother, first of all, who demonstrated what it means to love the Lord. In my younger days I didn't really appreciate that but I certainly do now. She prayed for me unfailingly during the questioning teenage years.

My wife, Anne, to whom I've now been married for 48 years. I've presented her with many challenges but she has loved me faithfully all these years, as I love her.

Iain Allan, to whom I have been for wise counsel many times. He taught me many important spiritual principles which have stood me in good stead through many years. I had the privilege of working with him for over five years as worship leader in the fellowship he pastored.

Peter Cochrane. Peter is someone with whom I've had a 'life link', as he terms it, for a number of years. More recently we've had closer fellowship which I've found to be very beneficial and encouraging. 'Iron sharpens iron.'

<u>Jim and Elizabeth Robertson</u>, whom I've known for many years. Their friendship and fellowship have been constant over a good number of years and they were among those who encouraged me to write this book. They also acted as our UK Home Agents when Anne and I spent two years each in China and the Philippines.

I should also mention many others, although not by name, who have contributed to my life and shown friendship. I'm grateful for their patience in putting up with my many foibles!

# About the author

During his 50+ years' walk with the Lord the author has served the Lord and the local church as musician, worship leader, teacher, Sunday School superintendant, elder, treasurer, prison ministry—and more, including service overseas in China and the Philippines.

This book comes out of his secret history with God.

Lightning Source UK Ltd.
Milton Keynes UK
UKOW05f0811181013

219262UK00001B/7/P